LET DAY BEGIN thrusts you into a rich study of Genesis, a book alive with message and meaning. It spans the time from Creation to the Flood, from the call of Abraham to the beginning of the nation of Israel. Studies in the Book of Job help amplify the two distinct themes of Genesis:

● We live in a **personal** universe—this world is the creative design of an infinite being.

● We live in a **purposive** universe—the creative God has provided for redemption.

Larry Richards' comprehensive treatment of the Beginnings takes us past what people say about the Bible and into what God is saying to us *through* the Bible.

LARRY RICHARDS
BIBLE ALIVE SERIES

Let Day Begin

Man in God's Universe
Studies in Genesis and Job

David C. Cook Publishing Co.
ELGIN, ILLINOIS—WESTON, ONTARIO
LA HABRA, CALIFORNIA

David C. Cook Publishing Co., Elgin, IL 60120

Printed in the United States of America

ISBN: 0-912692-87-1

ACKNOWLEDGMENTS

Special Acknowledgment is made to the following for permission to reprint copyrighted material:

The Division of Christian Education of the National Council of Churches of Christ in the U.S.A.: from the Revised Standard Version of the Bible. Copyrighted 1946, 1952, © 1971, 1973 by the D.C.E. of the National Council of Churches of Christ in the U.S.A.

The Lockman Foundation: from the *New American Standard Bible*. Copyright © 1960, 1962, 1963 Lockman Foundation.

The New York Bible Society International: from the *New International Version* of the Bible. Copyright © 1973 the New York Bible Society International.

Tyndale House Publishers: from *The Living Bible*. Copyright © 1971 Tyndale House Publishers.

Zondervan Publishing House: from *A Survey of Israel's History* by Leon Wood. Copyright © 1970 Zondervan Publishing House.

Quotations from the Bible are from the Revised Standard Version except where indicated otherwise.

ACKNOWLEDGMENTS

CONTENTS

LET DAY BEGIN

MYTH OR MESSAGE?

IN SOME SUNDAY SCHOOL LESSONS for older children, the writer tells them to look at parts of the Bible as myth, as "a story made up to explain something mysterious in the days when people knew nothing about science, and did not know the cause of things like mountains, or thunder."[1] According to this approach, much in the Old Testament is legendary or mythical, particularly in the Book of Genesis. Commenting on the Flood and rainbow, the writer dismisses the Flood story and explains the rainbow myth: "We know now what causes rainbows and we do not think of God as a warrior with a great war bow. But this story shows us how the Jews, a very long time ago, tried to explain this mysterious thing they sometimes saw in the sky."

To the above writer, the difficult elements of

1. Eric Lord, *What Is the Bible?* Readiness for Religion series. Ronald J. Goldman, ed. (New York: Morehouse-Barlow, 1971).

the Old Testament are to be viewed as myth or legend or as true-to-life, but made-up stories, like that of Jonah.

Such a view of the Bible is not unusual. If we start from the assumption that Scripture is best understood as a human groping after God, or even as the best insights of truly religious people, we must always hold open the possibility that the writers of Scripture were wrong, that their ideas are false, that their stories are not rooted in historical fact or that, at best, they are embellishments of heroic acts distorted by centuries of retelling. If we start with the assumption that Scripture is best understood as having originated in the minds and imaginations of men like you and me, then it's only right that we should see its dramatic tales as myth or legend. And it is only right that as we read we should trust our own judgment, not the wisdom of men who lived in that distant prescientific age.

But are the Scriptures simply human documents? Certainly the authors did not think of Old or New Testament writings as merely the thoughts of men. Over 2,600 times in the Old Testament alone the writers claim to be speaking or writing not their words, but God's! "The word of the Lord came to Jeremiah . . . . Thus saith the Lord . . . . Hear the word of the Lord." These men had no doubts about what they were reporting. They firmly believed that they recorded messages from God to man.

This is the view of the New Testament as well.

One passage says it very plainly. In I Corinthians 2: 9-13 we're told that God has communicated to us what we could never discover for ourselves or even imagine. God has revealed through His Holy Spirit the very thoughts of God!

This certainly was Jesus' view as well. He spoke of Creation and of the Flood, of Jonah and of the destruction of Sodom and Gomorrah, as historical events, not as myths. And He saw them as events that have a living message for men of every age.

Here is another striking difference that sets the Scriptures apart from the myths and legends that make up the folklore of other peoples. Not only are the sacred writings of the Jews seen as historically accurate and factual, not only are these documents which traced the heritage of Israel seen as divine revelation rather than human speculation, but these sacred writings are a *living* heritage. Through the Scriptures the God who spoke to men of old speaks to believers today.

In a very real sense, our heritage in God's Word is contemporary as well as historical. To understand the Word of God and be enriched by it, we have to approach the Bible as both truth to be understood and as a living word from God addressed to us "now."

The Old Testament record is our heritage too. It is the very root of our faith and of our understanding of God as He reveals Himself to men. The Old Testament is a vital part of our living heritage, a document designed by God to speak to you and me, and to transform our lives as we learn to respond to Him. This is what the apostle Paul refers to when he looks back at one Hebrew generation and says, "These things happened to them as examples and were written down as warnings for us, on whom the fulfillment of the ages has come" (I Cor. 10: 11, *New International Version)*. In the actual historical setting, God ministered to that ancient generation. In the record of those events, God ministers to us. In all that God did and said, in all that men of old experienced, we mine our own rich heritage. The Old Testament record was made and preserved across the millenniums for us.

NOT MYTH, MESSAGE

This, then, is the conviction I have as we begin with Genesis to explore the Old Testament—a conviction I hope you share, or will share, as we go on. Genesis, like the rest of Scripture, is God's message to us. It is historical, reporting events which actually happened in space and time, in the reality of our own universe. It is at the same time a focused revelation. The events recorded have been purposefully selected. The details included—and those left out—have been carefully chosen. The reasons behind the choice, the criteria of selection which gives the Old Testament its focus and which guides us in searching it, is the criteria of message. God through His Word is communicating with you and me.

This too sets the Bible apart. While what is re-

14

corded is history, it is more than history. The events recorded, God's mighty acts as He intervened in the world, show us who He is and tell us of His ways. And the Scriptures go beyond recording the facts; they explain in words the intentions and purposes, the emotions and concerns, which led God to His actions. In this way the Bible is an important blend; it shows us God in action, then reveals the motives underlying all God has done.

Noting this, we're brought face to face with yet another uniqueness. The Bible involves both *propositional revelation* (objective statements of truth expressed in words) and *personal revelation* (bringing us into contact with God Himself, not merely with ideas about Him). When we read of all God has done in history and discover His revealed thoughts and motives, God Himself confronts us as a Person. We meet Him; He speaks to us; He invites and commands our response. Through His Word we are drawn into a personal relationship with Him and, responding, we come to know Him in even closer, more personal, ways.

So the message of Scripture involves both the communication of truth about God and, at the same time, the message of Scripture is God Himself as a Person.[2] As you and I trace God's interaction with human beings across the centuries, we will come to know Him better. And we'll come to know Him well.

2. For an extended discussion of the relationship between propositional and personal revelation, see Larry Richards, *Creative Bible Study* (Chicago: Moody, 1970), chaps. 1-5.

We have special help for coming to understand and to know God. Not only do we have the record of God's gradual, progressive (spanning some 2,000 years) revelation of Himself to Israel. We also have the *completed* revelation. We have the perspective provided by the New Testament, the final, divine commentary which interprets for us the fullest meaning of all that happened in the Old. From the vantage point of Jesus' death and resurrection, we have the Holy Spirit's explanation of how He fulfills and completes realities that may only have been hinted at before He came. So as we trace the process of God's self-revelation through history, enlightened by the explanations found in the Old Testament and completed in the New, we can approach the study of the Word with confidence. Confidence that we will understand. Confidence that we will meet God Himself in His Word. Confidence that if we will hear His voice today, we will find and know our living heritage.

OUR PERSPECTIVE

Our perspective as we approach reading the Old Testament is important. If we look at what we read merely as dry stories of people long dead, we're likely to be bored. If we look at what we read as the interesting but irrelevant myths of an ancient tribal people, we're likely to find the Old Testament fun—but without meaning for us today.

What I've suggested so far is that our perspective as we approach the Old Testament needs to involve several unique understandings.

■ *The Old Testament is to be approached as the Word of God.* It is not a record of human speculation but of a divine, verbal (in words) revelation.

■ *The Old Testament is to be approached as a living history.* The events recorded are historical. But the record is designed to speak to you and me today.

■ *The Old Testament is to be approached as God's message.* Everything included is focused, selected to tell us about God and His intentions. We are to look for the message in the events.

■ *The Old Testament is to be approached as God's personal self-revelation.* We not only find truth about God in the Bible; we meet Him there face to face. We are to open our hearts to Him, eager to see Him, ready to respond when He speaks.

■ *The Old Testament is to be approached from the vantage point provided by Christ.* The New Testament is a divine commentary, helping us to understand the Old. We need to see the Old Testament as true, yet incomplete. And we need to look to the New Testament and to Jesus to bring the incomplete into perspective.

What happens if we take the stand of faith and adopt these perspectives as we approach our study of Genesis and the rest of the Old Testament?

What happens is that we discover our heritage. We find our identity in common with all who have trusted God and located the roots of their self-understanding in relationship with Him. We sink our roots deeply into the realization of who God

17

is. And, in the confidence provided by truly knowing God, we are strengthened to live each today
with joy. All this is our heritage.

Let's grasp it firmly and go on.

OUR HERITAGE IN GENESIS

Genesis, the first book of the Old Testament, is
extremely rich in message and meaning. It spans
the time from Creation, on through the cataclysmic event of the Flood, to the call of Abraham and
the formation of a distinct people, a people chosen
from among all mankind through whom God's
purposes are to be realized.

As its message, Genesis presents two strong and
distinct themes. The first, the emphasis of chapters 1-9, affirms that we live in a *personal universe.*
The physical universe is presented as the creation
and design of a Person. Human beings are seen as
distinct from all the rest of animate and inanimate
creation, shaped to fit within the framework of
both physical and spiritual reality. There is no hint
in Genesis of the pagan notion that personifies the
inanimate. Sun and moon are not "gods" who
created the earth or from whose substance animal
life sprang. There is the strongest denial of the
similar modern fiction that life somehow generates
itself spontaneously from nonliving matter and
gradually evolves from simple, single cells into the
complex and many forms of life we know today.

No, a personal God is set forth in Genesis as the
ultimate reality, distinct from and yet the ground

of being of all that exists. And every fact of existence is to be understood in the light of His personality and His purposes.

Hearing this message, we meet ourselves and find our destiny. We come to understand and to value ourselves as special to God, not merely one with the animals. As the objects of His love, we discover our identity and take our place as heirs of all that He has made.

This discovery of ourselves and our place in creation is a freeing and challenging experience. It is part of our heritage, a heritage we'll discover as we explore God's message to us in Genesis.

There is another message, an emphasis found in Genesis chapters 12—50. The second message is that we live in a *purposive universe*. The personal God who shaped all that exists remains involved! He gives His creation direction and purpose. God has a plan that gives shape and meaning to all of history, a plan that helps us understand ourselves and the human condition and that gives us security even when wars and crime and tragedy mar our contemporary world. Starting with this second message of the Book of Genesis, all of Bible history begins to take shape and form.

Coming to discover God's purpose, to see the plan take shape, is a rich part of our heritage in Genesis and a vital element in grasping our identity. Both these messages, with all their dynamic, transforming power, are ours in Genesis, a heritage we need to discover and to appropriate as our own.

An outline. In a sense, the two messages of Genesis give us an outline of the Old Testament. Genesis 1—11 records God's dealings with the human race as a whole, spanning the uncounted centuries from Creation to the call of Abraham. Here we not only discover our identity as persons special to God. Here too we see the impact of sin and the Fall, the necessity of judgment, and the promise of renewal. Genesis goes beyond the beginning God made with Adam and Eve to sketch a great falling away of fallen man, until the "wickedness of man was great . . . every imagination of the thoughts of his heart was only evil continually" (Gen. 6: 5). This condition led to the judgment of the Genesis Flood.

Another new beginning was made with Noah's family in a renewed and freshened world. But this beginning also led to failure as the succeeding generations again turned against God. Finally God acted to select out of all mankind a single man, a single family. One writer has rather poetically suggested that "humanity must be thought of as a vast stream from which God, in the call of Abram and the creation of the nation Israel, has but drawn off a slender rill, through which He may at last purify the great river itself."[3]

However poetic, the suggestion is accurate. God did choose this family and this people. God did determine to accomplish His purposes through them. In fact, the great bulk of the Old Testament

3. From notes on Gen. 12 in the Scofield Reference Bible by C. I. Scofield.

deals not with the thousands of years before the call of Abram, but with the 2,000 or more years from Abraham to Christ! Balanced against the 11 chapters of early Genesis are the 905 chapters remaining in the Old Testament's 39 books, chapters which further develop and expand the purposes initiated in that one called and chosen man.

We'll see more of these purposes as we move through the entire Old Testament to explore our heritage in them. But we can outline the purposes here; they stand out sharp and clear in Genesis.

1. *A redemptive purpose.* Israel was the womb from which Jesus, the promised seed and source of universal blessing, was to come. Salvation came through the Jews.

2. *A regal purpose.* God intends to establish His sovereign rule and His authority in this world. This purpose too is fulfilled in Jesus, the promised Messiah-King who, with a redeemed Israel, will reign over the whole earth.

3. *A revelatory purpose.* God revealed Himself to Israel, and through Israel to the world that then was. And in the Word given to Israel, God continues to reveal Himself to us. Through the Jewish people whom God chose to be His own has come our knowledge of God.

The Source. Where did the Genesis documents come from? How accurate can they be?

Obviously no writer stood beside God in Creation. No one observed the forming of Adam and Eve or watched as the world was destroyed in the surging waters of the Flood.

But Moses or his associates gave us a record.

In its written form, Genesis is associated with Moses and the Exodus from Egypt. Many Genesis incidents—dealing, for instance, with Abraham or Isaac or Joseph—were undoubtedly part of an oral tradition, stories by which the Jews transmitted their heritage from generation to generation. Fragments of what we now know as Genesis may have been recorded in writing. Archaeological evidence indicates that written records had been preserved for at least a millennium and a half before the Mosaic era. So it's likely Moses had access

FIGURE I **OVERVIEW OF THE OLD TESTAMENT**

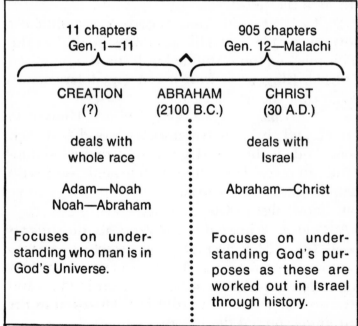

11 chapters Gen. 1—11		905 chapters Gen. 12—Malachi
CREATION (?)	ABRAHAM (2100 B.C.)	CHRIST (30 A.D.)
deals with whole race		deals with Israel
Adam—Noah Noah—Abraham		Abraham—Christ
Focuses on under-standing who man is in God's Universe.		Focuses on under-standing God's pur-poses as these are worked out in Israel through history.

to written records from antiquity. Yet the point remains clear: Much that is included could only be known by direct revelation. Even the meaning of the fragments of history and the oral traditions could only be interpreted by God the Holy Spirit. And so our confidence, like that of the Biblical writers themselves, must rest in the superintending ministry of the Holy Spirit who oversaw the whole process of selection and writing, and whose supernatural ministry stands today as the foundation of our confidence that the Bible's details and message both come to us as God intended they should.

Because of God, these ancient writings are today *our* heritage. Their message is to us. Let's enter into that heritage joyfully, eager to possess it fully and eager to let its truths possess us.

GOING DEEPER

to personalize

1. Jot down words that express how you've felt about the Old Testament in your previous reading of it. Whatever you've really felt (whether bored or excited!), write it down.

2. Look over the list of ways we are to approach Scripture to discover our heritage (see p. 17). Put a plus sign (+) beside each statement that portrays an attitude *you have had* when you've read the Old Testament. Put a minus sign (−) beside the statements that portray an attitude that you *have not had* when you've read the Old Testament.

Now look back at the "feeling" words you jotted down. What is the relation between your feelings about the Old Testament and the way you have approached it?

3. Finally, look over the summary of the two major messages of Genesis (pp. 18, 19). List ways these messages might be important to you. List questions you might have about them. Finally, write a brief statement: "God, from my study of this part of Your Word to me, I want _____."

to probe

1. Can we trust the Bible? If you're uncertain, do some research in books like these: René Pache, *The Inspiration and Authority of Scripture* (Chicago: Moody, 1970); Carl Henry, ed., *Revelation and the Bible* (Grand Rapids: Baker, 1958) or older classics like Benjamin Warfield, *The Inspiration and Authority of The Bible* (Nutley: Presbyterian and Reformed, 1948).

2. Using a concordance, check what the Old Testament claims for itself as to being "the Word of God." Write your conclusions in a short paper, quoting key passages.

3. Read through the Gospel of Matthew and note how the writer uses the Old Testament. Note particularly how Jesus speaks of the Old Testament. What view of the Old Testament does Jesus seem to hold?

HOW GREAT THOU ART

WE'RE WRONG IF WE THINK OF GENESIS 1 as the only place in the Bible where we meet God as the Creator. Far from being an early Hebrew myth, the Creation story is a vital part of continuing revelation. Both the Old and New Testaments affirm the essential integrity of all we read in Genesis 1. Both help us explore the meaning of the majestic affirmations about God and the world which we read at the beginning of our Bibles.

One of the most striking of these continuing themes is expressed in Isaiah: "For Jehovah created the heavens and earth and put everything in place, and he made the world to be lived in, not to be an empty chaos" (Isa. 45: 18, *The Living Bible).* The universe was created for a purpose: to be the home of man. However vast our expanding universe may be, it is living beings and not inanimate matter that are the focus of God's concern.

Psalms like the 104th review the creative act of

God and praise Him for forming mountain and valley and sea and stream as a habitation for man and for "living things both great and small." With heart full of wonder the psalmist realizes,

These all look to thee,
  to give them their food in due
    season.
When thou givest to them, they
    gather it up;
  when thou openest thy hand,
    they are filled with good
    things.
When thou hidest thy face, they are
    dismayed;
  when thou takest away their
    breath, they die
  and return to their dust.
When thou sendest forth thy Spirit,
    they are created;
  and thou renewest the face of the
    ground.

Psalm 104: 27-30

The psalmist concludes, "Praise God forever! How he must rejoice in all his work!" (Ps. 104: 31, TLB).

THE PERSONAL TOUCH

It's important as we read the familiar Creation story to approach it with the attitude of the psalmist. He recognizes God as Creator. He knows the story of the seven days; but as he meditates, his thoughts are not drawn off to a speculative "How?" Instead he quickly penetrates to the central message: All that exists is the work of a Person. Everything around us has been carefully and thoughtfully designed. Creation is a mirror placed to reflect our thoughts and our worship to the Person whose image Creation enables us to see.

This is the central message of Genesis 1. It is not told to direct our attention to the world, but to its Maker. The psalmist, recognizing this message, shouts, "I will sing to the Lord as long as I live. I will praise God to my last breath! May he be pleased by all these thoughts about him, for he is the source of all my joy" (Ps. 104: 33, 34, TLB).

A witness. The Old and New Testaments join in asserting that creation does give a compelling witness to God. Psalm 19 points out that the universe is a wordless message about God which anyone, whatever his language or education, can hear.

> The heavens are telling the glory
> of God;
> and the firmament proclaims his
> handiwork.
> Day to day pours forth speech,
> and night to night declares knowledge.
> There is no speech, nor are there words;
> their voice is not heard;
> yet their voice goes out through all
> the earth,
> and their words to the end of the world.
>
> *Psalm 19: 1-4*

The same point is made by Paul in the Book of Romans. But there Paul sees creation as giving evidence *against* unbelief! Paul argues that man's wickedness is revealed in his struggles to suppress the knowledge of God and refusing to accept the testimony of creation. "What may be known about God is plain to them," the Bible says, "because God has made it plain to them. For since the creation of the world God's invisible qualities—his eternal power and divine nature—have been clearly seen, being understood from what has been made, so that men are without excuse" (Rom. 1: 19, 20, NIV). Creation gives such compelling proof of God's existence and is such a clear reflection of His personality that all "wise" explanations designed to rule God out serve only to underline man's perversity.

And it is striking to trace man's attempts through the ages to explain creation apart from God. In the culture from which Abraham sprang, the ancients imagined that the material universe was rooted in a great waste of waters, sweet water and salt water, personified in myth as two gods, male and female. Creation began as intercourse between this pair; then war arose between the parents and the secondary gods, their children. One of the lesser gods killed the original father with little difficulty. But the original female was much more of a threat. However, the hero god, Marduk, was elected leader and overthrew her, ultimately shaping earth and sky from her dead body. The epic poem telling this story reports:

28

Then the lord paused to view her dead body.
That he might divide the monster and do artful
  works
He split her like a shellfish into two parts:
Half of her he set up and called it as sky.

For decades liberal scholars have noted slight similarities between this Babylonian myth and the Genesis Creation story. They suggested that the stories spring from a common heritage and share a common character. Yet Henry Frankfort, accurately observing the similarity between the world views of Babylonian and Egyptian cultures, notes that their fundamental assumptions were "in fact, universally accepted by the peoples of the ancient world *with the single exception of the Hebrews.*"[1]

In fact, the fundamental difference between the ancient concepts of Creation and the Scripture, which insists that God be viewed as the One who made the physical universe from nothing and is distinct from it, can hardly be explained as a common cultural heritage! Or by assuming that the Hebrews were wiser than those around them, or more holy. The Bible's teaching about God and Creation is explained simply by the fact that in His Word God speaks in order to cut through the distortions that mark fallen man's thinking about Him.

Even today, however, men continue their attempts to explain God away and to find a different

1. Henry Frankfort, *Before Philosophy* (Baltimore: Penguin Books, 1949), italics added.

29

face in the mirror of Creation. These attempts are a striking reversal of the Babylonian. While the ancients saw the physical universe as bodies of once living gods, the moderns try to explain life as coming from dead and inert matter! How could it have happened? Somehow in the great shallow seas, life, it is said, was spawned. Over the aeons, that life grew more complex. The single cell multiplied, differentiated into eye and lung and brain and blood and bone. Never mind the fact that biologists "know of no way other than random mutation by which new hereditary variation comes into being."[2] Ignore the fact that "there is a delicate balance between an organism and its environment which a mutation can easily upset," so that "one could as well expect that altering the position of the brake or gas pedal at random would improve the operation of an automobile."[3] Today, as in the ancient world, the urge persists to find an explanation for man and the universe, but an explanation which leaves out God.

But reason and revelation both bear witness. You and I live today in *God's* universe.

GOD OF THE UNIVERSE

Even the first few words of Genesis 1 introduce concepts vast in their sweep and power.

2. C. H. Waddington, in *The Nature of Life* (New York: Atheneum, 1961), p. 98.

3. Frederick S. Hulse, *The Human Species* (New York: Random House, 1963), p. 53.

"In the beginning." The Greeks had a cosmology of endless cycle. They thought the universe was born in fire, cooled to shape the world they knew, destined soon to flare up again, only to have the cycle endlessly repeat itself each 10,000 years. The life they knew was just another rerun of what had always been and what would be again.

But God affirms a beginning, a point in time at which an irreversible process began. An origin, back to which we must go if we are to ever grasp the nature of the world we live in, or the meaning of our lives.

"In the beginning, God." This too is a powerful concept. Unlike men who struggle to find the meaning of life within the limits of the physical universe, the Bible directs our thought beyond the origin of matter to a Person: God.

We can attempt to explain ourselves and life's meaning as the result of random surgings of a lifeless sea billions of years ago. But if we do, all possibility of purpose for our existence is gone. What meaning can there be in chance happenings in an impersonal universe? What meaning, when not only our individual lives flicker out after sparking briefly in the endless dark, but when mankind itself looks back to find its heritage a mindless past, and ahead sees only the certain dimming of our sun and the settling mantle of an endless cold?

But Genesis 1 affirms *God.* God, a Person with mind and emotion and the power of choice, existed before the beginning. And so the very character of the universe shifts and changes before our eyes. The ultimate reality is not the random motion of dead, impersonal matter. The ultimate reality is a living, personal being. Life, not death, is the eternal ground of all that is.

You and I can find no meaning in a life that has root in the chance interplay of mindless atoms. But we can find meaning in a life that is now seen to be rooted in the action of another living personality. If God exists, and God is the cause of the material world, then we can look for meaning in His purposive act of Creation!

"In the beginning God created." Here we find a special sense of comfort and joy. God did act, freely and from His own choice, to create. There *is* purpose.

This is a particularly important thought. The Deists of 18th-century England, like the Auca of modern-day South American jungles, had the notion of a "watchmaker God." They saw God as someone who wound up the universe like a clock, and then left it, ticking, to run down, as he wandered off on other business, unconcerned about the toy he'd formed. But in Genesis 1 the introduction of the creative act implies far more. The complexity of the creation, the care which God took in shaping it and the purpose and design revealed, portray a God who acted with a distinct purpose in mind.

"In the beginning God created the heavens and the earth" (Gen. 1: 1). Here the final introductory note is sounded. God stands behind it all. The God of Genesis is no Platonic demiurge who, like a potter,

merely shaped an already existing clay. The living God does not share His eternity with rock, or even with the billion stars that span our sky. The source of all, the only and the ultimate reality, is God.

I've shared these few thoughts, not because I intend to give a commentary on each verse and phrase of Genesis 1, but to show how important it is not to pass on too quickly. We've read or heard these words a hundred times. Our very familiarity with them may blind us to the fact that this chapter, from its first words, expresses truths as powerful as any we might imagine.

We are not dealing here with "primitive myth." We're listening to the thoughts, the revelations, of God. We are invited into His mind and heart to find a clear expression of the deepest issues with which men can be concerned. And so we need to read and listen well.

I suggested earlier that the Bible pictures Creation as a mirror, a mirror that reflects the person of God. Certainly this is true in the Creation story. In the first few words God wipes away the mists that cloud the mirror and commands us to look at Him. "In the beginning God created the heavens and the earth."

What will we see as we go on through this chapter, looking closely into the mirror to glimpse His features?

We'll see many things that tell us about God. We'll see, for instance, that God is a God of order. Isaiah says, "He made the world to be lived in, not to be an empty chaos" (Isa. 45: 18, TLB). Many have noted patterns within the days of Creation. For instance, Joseph Free notes the orderly progression of the process:[4]

1st day: light	4th day: light-bearers
2nd day: firmament	5th day: marine and aerial life
3rd day: dry land	6th day: land animals, man

Charles Pfeiffer suggests this pattern:[5]

Work of division	Works of quickening and adorning
1st day: light	4th day: sun, moon, stars
2nd day: air and sea	5th day: birds, fish
3rd day: land, planets	6th day: animals and man

However we want to express it, it is clear that in the Creation account there are distinct sequences and order. Chaos and randomness are rejected.

Several patterns in Genesis 1 are tremendously revealing about who God is and what He is really like.

Differentiation. Often the text says, "and God separated," as "God separated the light from the darkness" (vs. 4). The Hebrew word here means "to make a distinction between." Light from dark, earth from seas, day from night—God established a pattern for the universe.

Dominion. Priority is also part of the created uni-

4. Joseph P. Free, *Archaeology and Bible History* (Wheaton, Ill.: Scripture Press, 1969).

5. Charles F. Pfeiffer, ed., *The Biblical World: A Dictionary of Biblical Archaeology* (Grand Rapids: Baker, 1966).

verse. Genesis 1 speaks of rule and dominion. There is a difference in function and purpose in creation, and some functions have higher value and priority.

Diversity. The vast complexity and many forms of inanimate matter and life are also revealing. From the uniqueness of each snowflake to the individuality shown in the animal world, God's delight in creative expression and concern for the individual is shown.

Dependability. Through it all, the alternation and pulse between night and day, season and season, clearly reveal the consistency of God.

And we hear God's judgment: "It was good." In the pattern of the universe we discover a God whom we can trust because God *cares.* He is not changeable or capricious. God *values* and, in valuing, chooses to do that which is in every way nothing else but good.

Finally Genesis 1 has a climax. Creation has a purpose beyond the pleasure of God. Creation is an expression of love, designed that God might give it as a gift to the highest creative expression of all: man. And so the text tells us that God created man in His own image (a teaching we'll explore in the next chapter), and determined that man should have dominion over all He had made. And so the repeated words to Adam, "I have given you . . ." stand as a benediction to this initial word. A benediction that marks God as One who cares for others, a first dim indication that the God with whom we have to do is love.

"BUT, GOD . . ."

I suppose it isn't strange that when we read the first chapter of Genesis we find it hard to recapture the mood of the psalmist. We see the problems, the questions we want answered. We react to God's great affirmation about Himself and our universe with the puzzled cry, "But, God, what about the 24-hour days? And, when did Creation take place?"

The days. There have been many speculations, trying to relate Genesis 1 to what we think we know about the age of the universe. The central ones about the days are:

1. The gap theory. This suggests an original creation of order and beauty, ruined by Satan's fall, with Genesis 1 describing a reconstruction. The name comes from the proposed ages-long gap between Genesis 1: 1 (God created) and Genesis 1: 2 (the earth was chaos).

2. The indefinite age theory. This suggests that the term "day" is figurative; that, in fact, the creative activity of each day covers geologic eras. The day in which man appeared has not yet ended.

3. The creation *in situ* theory. This suggests a creation in 24-hour days a short time ago. Coal, petroleum and fossils were created in place. The history in the fossil records is only "apparent."

4. The revelatory day theory. This suggests that God revealed His work to Moses in seven literal days. It is the days of Moses' experience that are marked with evening and morning in Genesis.

5. The revelatory device theory. This suggests the human author simply used "days" to organize his material. The facts are true, but not the framework.

6. The myth theory. This, the first theory not held by orthodox believers, suggests that the passage is not historical in any sense, but symbolic instead. It contains only "theological" truths, not history.

There are many books and articles that argue for first one and then another of these theories. But the fact is that the text of Genesis and the doctrine of revelation do not seem to demand that we reject any except the last. Our curiosity is not satisfied. God seems to insist we look beyond the "how" to Him.

Dating. Dating the Creation has likewise generated endless speculation. Some 300 years ago an Irish bishop, Ussher, by studying the genealogies of Genesis, computed the date of Creation as 4004 B.C. By 1738, over 200 known attempts to compute the date ranged from 3483 B.C. to 6984 B.C.!

These attempts at dating assumed that the genealogies of the Bible were complete and overlooked the Hebrew way of compressing genealogies. For instance, look at Matthew 1: 8 in which Joram is said to beget Uzziah, his great-great-grandson, and Ezra 7: 3, in which six generations are omitted. Clearly the terms "son of" and "beget" are used in Hebrew literature in the sense of "descendant" and "progenitor."

Other approaches to dating also fall short, including modern radiocarbon methods. We can accept the Carbon 14 dates (although there is an increasing doubt about C-14 authority) for Middle East cultural artifacts at 7,000-10,000 years B.C. And, accepting them, still know no more about the cosmic time scale and have no better answer to the question of when Creation took place.

Somehow Genesis does not seem concerned with the kind of questions we like to raise. It is enough for the writer to affirm God, and portray man as living now in God's universe.

And, perhaps it should be enough for us as well, for Genesis 1 invites us to turn our gaze, not to our gadgets and our instruments and our deductions, but to God. And, seeing God the Creator, to cry, "How great Thou art!"

GOING DEEPER

to personalize

1. From Genesis 1 record all the insights you can gain into God's personality and character. What, in addition to differentiation, dependability and valuing, do His actions show?

2. Explore passages in which Bible writers respond to God as Creator (Pss. 148; 104; Job 38; Isa. 40, etc.). How are you and I to respond to Genesis 1?

3. The New Testament reveals Jesus was the active Agent in Creation (Jn. 1: 1-5; Col. 1: 15-20). Read Genesis 1, substituting Jesus' name for

"God." Does this help you see Creation as a personal and loving act?

4. Respond in some appropriate way to God as Creator (perhaps in art, song, poetry or whatever). How might you express your appreciation to our great God?

to probe

1. Read several views about the days of Creation.

2. Examine some of the many books that discuss the age of the earth. Be sure to check those by theologians and Christian scientists as well.

3. Look up the Babylonian creation story, and compare it directly with Genesis 1 (see books on archaeology and the Bible).

4. List major conflicts between evolutionist and creationist views. What kinds of evidence are advanced by both sides?

5. Look up the word "create" in a concordance which lists original languages (Strong's or Young's are good). What can you learn about God's creative actions through such a study?

6. The materialist is likely to see the universe as "the great tomb of man" *(Thanatopsis)*. But the believer is more likely to see the universe as a great garden of life. How does Genesis 1 help explain the reason behind the differing viewpoints?

THE NAKED APE?

NOT LONG AGO A BOOK entitled *The Naked Ape* was given considerable attention. It was an attempt to explain human behavior by comparing similarities between man and simian, and the author suggested that modern man's ills come from culture, the rejection of primitive reaction for socially programmed response. It was quickly followed by a book by a feminist who resented the ape tradition in anthropology because it made man the hunter and woman a servant. She solved that problem by arguing that humanity evolved from a dolphinlike progenitor; in the setting of the seas, male and female roles would have been the same! These books introduced nothing new in the long history of speculation about man's origins. Thales, a Greek philosopher who lived centuries before Christ, had already propounded the dolphin theory, suggesting man had evolved from these intelligent mammals of the sea. And the supposed descent from simianlike ancestors has provided psychologists with a rich field for speculation. Particularly this supposed heritage was viewed as the source of a "vast, subconscious will, that acts out of a monstrous irrationality—an irrationality that has made it evolve its own enemy, rational consciousness."[1] This picture of the untamed animal in man lurking beneath the thin and weak veneer of civilization is a desperate one, but one accepted by evolutionists. It seems to them to explain the tragic ways in which human beings so often behave. The hatred, the brutality, the crime, the strange selfishness and propensity to hurt even those we love, make sense to those who find the identity of man in some distant, mindless brute.

THE GOOD

It's fascinating to realize that man's search for origins is organized around a probing for the reason for evil in humanity. Few seem compelled to explain the good. Yet the good is far more difficult to understand. If the roots of human behavior are imbedded deeply in some "great invisible octopus writhing in the depths of the mind," then what is the evolutionary source of love? Of appreciation for truth and beauty? Of a sense of responsibility for others? Of altruism, and the willingness to sacrifice? Where is the source of man's curiosity and creativity? Where is the spring of

1. Colin Wilson, *New Pathways in Psychology* (New York: Taplinger, 1972), p. 95.

thought and reason, of the ability and the desire to value? And how do we explain that universal awareness that there is something beyond, an awareness that expresses itself even in the most isolated cultures in some kind of worship? How do we explain the serving—or placating—of the supernatural?

It's strange that the believer has been cast as hung up on sin. In fact it is the man who rejects God whose every attempt to understand himself seems to draw him inexorably to struggle with the awesome gap he sees between what man feels he ought to be—and what he is.

Scripture is different. Yes, it recognizes the fact of sin. But the Bible insists that you and I see our origins and explain our essential natures as springing from an earlier source. In fact, the Bible insists that you and I begin our search for our identity by affirming, with God, that we bear the image of the Lord and not the image of the ape—the image of the Creator and not the image of the Missing Link.

This teaching, which we meet first in Genesis 1 and 2, is not isolated to these passages. After the fall, God instituted capital punishment for murder as the ultimate crime. For murder is taking the life of a person made in God's image (Gen. 9: 5, 6). In the New Testament James points out the inconsistency involved in blessing God and, with the same voice, cursing men "who are made in the likeness of God" (Jas. 3: 9).

Even more striking is the meditation of David in Psalm 8:

43

When I look at thy heavens, the work
  of thy fingers,
 the moon and the stars which thou
   hast established;
 what is man that thou art mindful of him,
 and the son of man that thou dost
   care for him?
Yet thou hast made him little less
  than God,
 and dost crown him with glory and
   honor.
Thou hast given him dominion over
  the works of thy hands;
 thou hast put all things under his feet.

Hebrews 2 comments on this psalm: "In putting everything under him [man], God left nothing that is not subject to him. Yet at present we do not see everything subject to him" (Heb. 2: 8, NIV). What we do see, Hebrews goes on to say, is Jesus. Jesus, who died, is now crowned with glory and honor. And through His death Jesus has succeeded in "bringing many sons to glory" (vs. 10, NIV). In this great New Testament passage God recognizes the gap between man's intended destiny and his experience, and God affirms man's value. You and I are still so important to God that He sent His Son to share in our humanity (see Heb. 2: 14, NIV). You and I are still so important that Jesus died to free us from slavery and to restore the glory and the dominion our heritage demands.

As J. B. Phillips paraphrases it, "It is plain that for this purpose he [Christ] did not become an angel; he became a man" (Heb. 2: 16). Man was at Creation, and man remains today, just as special.

THE IMAGE

The Genesis 1 portrait of man's creation and the days before the fall provides the foundation for our understanding of ourselves.

Dominion. There are many things in Genesis 1: 26-31 that are exciting. For instance, the interplay in God's words about Himself is fascinating. "Let *us* make man in our image," God said, and so "in the image of God . . . *he* created them." Here is the first hint of Trinity, the first faint indication that God is one, yet somehow plural in His unity. In these verses too are the roots of the Christian's concern for ecology. The earth and all its creatures were given into man's keeping. To us then came both the gift and the responsibility.

In these verses too is the first affirmation of the essential rightness of sex. Far from supporting the old notion that the original sin was sexual intercourse between Adam and Eve, God before the fall commanded them to "be fruitful and multiply, and fill the earth and subdue it" (1: 28). It was God who created us "male and female" (vs. 27). It was God who designed human sexuality and, looking at *"everything* that he had made," pronounced it "very good" (vs. 31).

As significant as these things are, it's clear that

45

the Genesis 1 account of man's creation stresses two messages. One of them is this: Man was created to have dominion. God shared His authority with man and, in the sharing, God gave man the privilege of responsibility.

This mantle of dominion settles over us as a dynamic reversal of all we have thought ourselves to be. Too often you and I feel a helplessness and impotence that drain us of the will to act. All too commonly we are overwhelmed by the vast impersonality of circumstance, overcome by the feeling that we are unable to struggle upstream against events we cannot control. With modern apostles of despair, we feel like bits of flotsam tossed on surging seas. But the Bible insists that you and I have a different heritage! A heritage in Creation that restores our confidence to meet and master circumstance. Only God is our Master. And in His plan we have been shaped to have dominion over all.

Certainly sin has robbed us of the full experience of dominion. Sin enslaves us. But Hebrews 2 cries out that through Jesus' death you and I have been freed (vs. 15)! Freed to taste again, in our personal experience, the meaning of dominion. Freed to live beyond circumstances, we are once again in relationship with God and once again in control.

Imago dei. The other message of the Creation story, *imago dei* (God's image), explains our dominion. God could give man this gift because God has shaped man to be like Him.

There is a long history of debate concerning the nature of the "image of God." In what respect did God make man like Himself? Some have felt the key to likeness was an original holiness. But even after the fall, the image persists (Gen. 9: 6; Jas. 3: 9). And the New Testament makes it clear that the holiness Adam had was lost and only now is being renewed in us by Christ (Eph. 4: 24; Col. 3: 9-11). So most commentators have agreed that the uniqueness of man is the key to understand image. Man and man alone shares with God all the attributes of personhood.

We know from the Bible that God values, has emotions, chooses, appreciates beauty, demonstrates creativity, distinguishes between right and wrong, loves and even sacrifices Himself for the sake of others. We know from the Bible that God is a Person, with identity and individuality.

These attributes constituting personhood mark men off from the rest of creation! In fact, all those elements of good which are found in man must have their source in likeness to the divine! How utterly foolish men are to insist that the root of evil can be seen in a heritage from beasts, and never to realize that the explanation for good must be found in our heritage from God.

But this is the message of God's Word. Man comes from God. All the things on which we pride ourselves are ours because of this original heritage all men share.

"So God created man in his own image, in the image of God he created him; male and female he

47

created them" (Gen. 1: 27). As a reflection of the Creator, each person is precious to God. As bearer of God's image, each person is worth even the price of redemption. You and I can never again look at others, or at ourselves, as valueless or base. We bear the image of God. And we are important to Him.

GENESIS 2

It's popular in some circles to think of Genesis 2 as a second, somewhat contradictory, account of Creation. In fact, Genesis 2 employs a common literary device. Background is sketched, and then one feature is highlighted with additional details. A choir sings, then one singer steps forward into the spotlight. A guide exposes the panorama of a giant mural and then leads his tour closer to examine the detail.

There is every indication that this is what we have in Genesis 2. The phrase in verse 4, "these are the generations of," sets off the introduction of each new section in Genesis (5: 1; 6: 9; 10: 1; 11: 10, 27; 25: 12, 19; 36: 1, 9; 37: 2). The Creation scenery is set in place in chapter 1; now the writer invites us to take our seats and to observe the play.

Special. Looking closely at chapter 2, we see many evidences that man truly is special to God. These are found primarily in the record of how God planned Eden to match the various needs of Adam's personality.

Remember that God's own personality was mirrored in Adam. With God, Adam shared a capacity to appreciate. So the plantings of Eden included every tree "that is pleasant to the sight" (vs. 9). God knew that man would be dissatisfied without work, so in the garden God let Adam "till it and keep it" (vs. 15). God knew man's need for opportunity to use his intellectual capacities, so God brought the animals to the man "to see what he would call them; and whatever the man called every living creature, that was its name" (vs. 19). God knew man's need for freedom to choose, so He placed a forbidden tree in the garden and commanded man not to eat fruit from it. This action once for all set man apart from programmed robots and demanded that he use his capacity to value and to choose. God knew man's need for intimacy with others of his kind, so God gave Adam and Eve to each other (vs. 22). And, finally, God knew man's need for fellowship with Him. So God gave Adam and Eve His own presence as the evenings fell (3:8).

Each of these actions show how deeply concerned God was that man's needs be met, and how special man, this being who was "in his own image" (1: 27), was to Him. In the design of Eden, God continued to reveal the fact that His own nature is one of love.

There are many ways in which we might respond to this witness to the special place man has in God's heart. For one, we might worship, echoing the wonder of the psalmist, "What is man, that

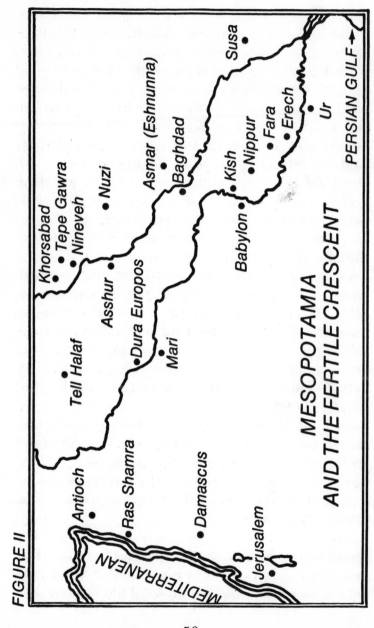

FIGURE II

MESOPOTAMIA AND THE FERTILE CRESCENT

50

thou art mindful of him?" (Ps. 8: 4).

For another, we might take comfort. The God whose care we see exhibited here still cares for you and me today. "In everything God works for good with those who love him," adds Romans 8: 28. God still designs experiences as loving gifts to those whom He holds dear.

For another response, we might take heart. "If God be for us," the Romans passage continues, "who can be against us?" (vs. 31, KJV). When God has affirmed us as His own concern, no circumstance can overcome. Dominion, still a gift from Him, *is* ours.

New life. The Genesis account makes it plain that man is a special creation, not a being whose flesh was formed from brutes, with the spark of likeness added as an afterthought. The picture in Genesis 2 shows God kneeling in tenderness to mold fresh clay. Then God breathes His own breath into that shape, and "man became a living being" (2: 7). Both the material and the immaterial dimensions of the human personality come from God, combined in a unique blend. And that blend will persist through all eternity, as ultimately you and I share both the shape and the character of Christ, who unites God with man in His own person.

Eden. What is important about Eden is the care God took in its design and what this tells us about ourselves and about Him. What we usually ask about Eden is, "Where was it?" Two of the rivers mentioned in the Biblical text are well known, so this has led scholars to suggest the narrowing

51

above Babylon, or further south near the Persian Gulf, as likely sites.

While archaeologists have agreed that the Fertile Crescent area is the focus of the most ancient and advanced civilizations on earth, there is no way today to pinpoint the location of Eden.

Woman. When we turn again to Scripture, the focus remains on Genesis 2 and its messages.

One of the most important messages has to do with the identity of women. This is something we are all concerned about these days, and with good reason. In Church and society, women's identity has been clouded with a variety of myths. Popular notions often project girls as more suggestible than boys, as having less self-esteem, as lacking motivation to achieve, as less aggressive and certainly as less analytic.[2] Tragic misunderstandings of Scripture have led some to affirm an actual inferiority of women on supposed religious grounds. Not only does this violate the spirit of Ephesians 5, in which man's headship is associated not with the right to command but with the responsibility of love, but it totally misses the implications of the Genesis Creation account.

What do we see in Genesis 2? We see first a deep need for woman as someone designed to fit the emptiness in man's life ("a helper fit for him," vs. 20). To fill the need, God did not turn again to clay. If He had, man might later have imagined

2. Eleanor E. Maccoby and Carol N. Jacklin, "Myth, Reality and Shades of Gray: What We Know and Don't Know About Sex Differences," *Psychology Today,* Dec. 1974, p. 109.

that woman, as a second creation, was somehow inferior to him. No, God put man to sleep and, while Adam rested, took a rib from him. Working His great wonders, from that rib God shaped Eve. When God brought Eve to Adam, he recognized her, and the words of Genesis 2:23 stand as a witness to the essential identity of woman with man:

> This at last is bone of my bones
> and flesh of my flesh;
> she shall be called Woman,
> because she was taken out of Man.

When God sought fellowship, He created man in His own image. But when this person God had made knew a similar need for intimacy, God gave an even greater gift. Woman, taken from the living flesh of man, is far more than a reflection of man's image. Woman, taken from the living flesh of man, shares fully in man's identity. In a testimony echoed by the New Testament, the Word of God lifts man and woman and places them, side by side, at the pinnacle of God's creation. There, together, each shares fully as a fellow heir of the dominion God proclaims, each a choice and precious object of His love.

GOING DEEPER

to personalize

(choose one or more of the following)
1. From Genesis 1 and 2 only, write on "God's plan for man."

2. From Genesis 1 and 2 only, develop a short "Biblical psychology." That is, explore how we are to understand persons and their needs, drives, capacities and fulfillments. There are more clues in Genesis 2 than the author has included under "special" on pages 48, 49.

3. From Genesis 2 write a statement about "The value of women."

4. From Genesis 1 and 2 only, write a paper on "Me: a person of worth and value."

5. Select one of the above areas and, in 500 words, record "What this truth means to me personally."

to probe

1. Study the concept of "dominion" ("rule"), using a concordance to locate key Bible passages.

2. Do an in-depth study of Hebrews 2. What does this New Testament passage say about (a) man as he was created, (b) man as redeemed, (c) our present relationship with God through Christ?

3. Study key Bible passages about women in the New Testament, and then compare them with this core passage in Genesis 2. How can you reconcile the affirmation of equality and identity with differences of function? How can you reconcile it with the limitation placed on women as to Church leadership?

4. How might Genesis 2 be used in marriage counseling? Work up a one- or two-session counseling approach.

THE REIGN OF DEATH

WITH GENESIS 3 THERE COMES a shattering of the idyllic picture of man in Eden. With a sudden jolt the harmony of original Creation is torn with discord; a wild cacophony of sounds among which we can hear notes of anger, jealousy, pride, disobedience, murder and the accompanying inner agonies of pain and shame and guilt. God's creation of man as a person stands as the source of good in us; now we face the source of evil.

We meet the specter early, in Genesis 2. To give man freedom to be a responsible moral being, God placed a certain tree in the center of the garden and commanded man not to eat. With the command came a warning of the consequences: "The day that you eat of it you shall die" (vs. 17). This opportunity to choose was no trap, or even a test. Given the intention of God that man should be in His image, it was a necessity! There is no moral dimension to the existence of a robot; it can only respond to the program of its maker. There is no capacity to value, to choose between good and bad, or good and better. To be truly like God, man must have freedom to make moral choices however great the risk such freedom may involve.

Daily Adam and Eve may have passed that tree, gladly obeying a God they knew and trusted. Until finally a third being stepped in.

SATAN

Scripture portrays a host of living, intelligent beings with personality and individuality called angels: "messengers." Some of these rebelled against God, and it is from this cosmic rebellion that evil has its origin, and from this source that the demons we read of in both Testaments have come.

At the top of the hierarchy of the rebellious angels is Satan. One interpretation would equate Satan with the Lucifer of Isaiah 14: 12 whose rebellion is so graphically portrayed:

> I will ascend to heaven;
>   above the stars of God
> I will set my throne on high . . .
> I will make myself like the Most High.
> *Isaiah 14: 13, 14*

This rebellion against the order established by God brought judgment, and Lucifer, with a great number of angelic beings who followed him, was judged in a titanic fall. His name was changed to Satan, and his arrogance became an unending hatred of God.

And it was this same being, this great adversary of God and His people, who came in the morning of the world in the guise of a serpent to tempt Eve.

The temptation (3: 1-7). It is fascinating to note the strategy of the tempter. First he isolated Eve from Adam. He gave the pair no opportunity to strengthen each other in a resolve to choose the good (cf. Heb. 10: 24, 25). Then he cast doubt on God's motives. Did God possibly have a selfish motive for the restriction (vs. 4)? Satan also contradicted God. God had warned of death; Satan cried, "That's a lie!" Now two opposing views stood in sharp contrast, and a choice had to be made.

Satan also focused Eve's attention on desirable ends, a common device of what is called today "situation ethics." Never mind the fact that the means to that end involve disobedience to God. Act only on examination of the supposed results. Satan also proposed a mixed good as the end: "You will become like him, for your eyes will be opened—you will be able to distinguish good from evil!" (vs. 5, TLB). How could becoming more like God be bad? Finally, Satan relied on the appeal of the senses. The fruit was "lovely and fresh looking" (vs. 6, TLB). How could anything that looks and tastes so pleasant be wrong?

Led along by the tempter, Eve made her choice.

She rejected trust and God and confidence in His wisdom and, as Satan had before her, determined to follow her own will. Then she shared the fruit with Adam, and he too ate.

And then, suddenly, the pair knew what they had done. They *did* know good and evil. But, unlike God, their knowledge came from an experience of the wrong! With opened eyes they looked at each other and, for the first time, closed their eyes in shame.

Death. When God set that single tree to stand as a testimony to man's freedom, He had warned, "The day that you eat of it you shall die" (2: 17). That day had come. Now death began to reign.

It is important to realize that much more than cessation of physical life is involved in the Biblical concept of death. Death in Scripture involves not only a return to dust but also distortion of the divine order, the warping of personality and relationships and alienation from God and His ways. Ephesians describes men's state apart from Christ as "dead in your transgressions and sins, in which you used to live when you followed the ways of this world and of the ruler of the kingdom of the air, the spirit [Satan] who is now at work in those who are disobedient. All of us also lived among them at one time, gratifying the cravings of our sinful nature and following its desires and thoughts" (Eph. 2: 1-3, NIV). Romans portrays the universal reign of death and sin, and insists, "There is no one righteous, not even one" (Rom. 3: 10, NIV; cf. vss. 9-18).

The implications of the first man's sin are traced in Bible passages like Romans 5: 12-21. Adam had been created in God's image. Then came the choice and, with it, death. The human personality was warped and marred. The image, dimmed and twisted now, remained. But man was ruled by death and all that death implies. What heritage had Adam to pass on? Only what he was. He fathered a son in his image, like Adam in worth because of correspondence to the divine, but like him also in his chains. "Therefore," the Bible says, "just as sin entered the world through one man, and death through sin, in this way death came to all men, because all sinned" (5: 12, NIV). The history of mankind is the dark record of the rule of death and stands as a grim testimony to the truth of God. What God warned Adam of did happen. And what God says to us today, in warning or in invitation, has that same certainty.

Demonstration of death. In looking at the message of Genesis 3 and 4 it is important to see that each detail is purposefully given. The principle of selection in these chapters seems clear: God is concerned that you and I understand the seriousness of sin and the fact of death. The series of events included provides an unmistakable demonstration of the death principle operating in human experience.

■ We see it in the sudden flush of shame that spread as Adam and Eve recognized their nakedness (3: 7). Today the more "mature" defend public nakedness as morally neutral. "Evil is in the eye

59

of the beholder" is the phrase they use to attack the objector, never realizing how true and how condemning this excuse is. Evil *is* in the eye of the beholder, not in the creation of God. But since the fall, evil describes the eye!

■ We see the death principle demonstrated in the first pair's flight from God. They had known His love, yet awareness of guilt alienated them from Him and they tried to hide (3: 8, 9).

■ We see it in Adam's refusal to accept responsibility. He tries to shift the blame to Eve, and ultimately to God: "It was the woman you gave me who brought me some" (3: 12, TLB).

■ We see death in the judgment on earth for man's sake (3: 17-19).

■ But most of all we see death in the anger of Cain, whose bitterness led him to murder Abel (4: 8). How deeply that tragedy must have driven home to Adam and Eve the implications of their choice. Father and mother must have stood in tears, gazing at the fallen body of one son, knowing only too well that the hand of their older boy was crimson with his blood.

■ We see death in the civilization that sprang up as the family of man multiplied. Lamech broke the pattern of relationship between man and woman that God ordained: "The two [shall] become one flesh" (Gen. 2: 24, NEB; 4: 19). Not only a bigamist, Lamech boldly justified a murder by pointing out that the other man had injured him.

Actually, we hardly need repeated proofs. Each day's headlines bring us continued testimony. The wrong we choose, the guilt and shame we bear, the way we strike out to hurt and harm, are ever-present, internal witnesses to Eden's loss. Yes, how well man knows good and evil now! With that first choice the power to experience the truly good was lost. We know the good, but only as an ideal, a yearning desire. We know the meaning of evil far more intimately. And we join with Paul in the lament, "What I want to do I do not do, but what I hate I do" (Rom. 7: 15, NIV). The longer we live, the stronger the realization grows: Paradise is lost.

THE RECOVERY OF HOPE

While Genesis 3 and 4 are among the most poignant chapters in the Bible, they do not leave us without hope. We find hope in God's action to clothe the naked pair in animal skins, the first intimation that for redemption blood must be shed. That first blood speaks of sacrifice, and sacrifice speaks of Christ.

We find hope in God's action in seeking out the sinning pair. Sin distorts our idea of God, erecting a grim barrier we're unwilling to approach. But God came into the garden, just as later Jesus would come into our world, to seek and to save those who were lost.

We find hope in the promise of God that an Offspring of the woman would destroy the serpent. Here, too, we see the glimmering prospect of the Incarnation, and the Savior's victory over death.

61

We also find hope as we trace through Scripture some of the theological concepts introduced in chapters 3 and 4. In fact, these chapters stand almost unmatched as seedbeds for basic truths about ourselves in God's universe—a universe we too have shaped, through sin.

Sin. One of the themes introduced here is human sin. The concept will continue to be developed through the revelation of the Old Testament and the New. Many different words will be used to describe the perverse twist that sin has introduced into human experience.

One set of Bible words portrays sin as missing the mark, as "falling short."

Another set of Bible words portrays sin as willful acts, the conscious choosing of known wrongs, using words like *transgress, trespass, go astray,* and *rebellion.* Both ideas are found here in Genesis 3. Adam and Eve fell short of God's requirements. They did so by obeying rationalized desire rather than obeying the command of God.

And so the human predicament is summed up, and with it, man's dilemma. Sin not only blinds us and leaves the good beyond our grasp, but sin also twists our will, moving us to desire and to choose what we know is wrong. Lost in impotence, men do not even desire to be truly free!

How is this revelation of sin a word of hope? In this: By sketching for us how complete our ruin is, God calls us to look away from ourselves, to Him.

Have you ever thought how striking the portrait of Cainitic culture is (4: 19-22)? This is no subsistence-level economy, struggling in primitive poverty to scratch a meager living from the ground. The text portrays division of labor and the taming of animals to man's use. We see culture. There is time for leisure, music and the arts. There is a technical competence that involves the smelting of ores and the development of metallurgy in bronze and iron. There is no suggestion here that the fall limited the ability of man to function effectively in this world. Instead, what we see is that no matter what progress man makes technologically, the underlying moral fault is unrepaired! Men can master the environment. But men cannot master themselves. We are competent to deal with our physical needs, but not to deal with the deepest needs of the human heart. Sin has warped the moral fabric of our universe, and only by looking to God to cover and transform, can man be saved.

Ultimate salvation. It's good to trace the story of sin through Scripture because in so doing we find the ultimate solution. For acts of willful sin, Christ's blood has won forgiveness. For our impotence, the Holy Spirit's presence brings wisdom and new power. For our final destiny, resurrection promises removal of the last vestiges of sin. Even the earth, which shares the curse (3: 17), will know renewal. In a poetic passage the New Testament reveals that the very "creation waits in eager expectation for the sons of God to be revealed. For the creation was subjected to frustration, not by its own choice, but by the will of the one who subjected it, in hope that the creation itself will be liberated from its bondage to decay and brought into the glorious freedom of the children of God" (Rom. 8: 19-21, NIV). The groaning world itself will know a liberation day when you and I are at last freed by God's great sacrifice from all that death and sin involve.

This is our destiny, and this our hope. One day the fullness of God's image will be restored.

AVENUES TO EXPLORE

So far we've looked only at the central message of Genesis 3 and 4. Sin *is* real; death is the common experience of the human race; only God's intervention offers hope.

But there are many additional riches in these chapters. Just a few of the areas of interest are:

The forbidden tree (2: 9). The importance of the tree was not in the nature of its fruit, but in the choice of man to listen to God's Word or to disobey. Paul asserts that "nothing is intrinsically unholy" (Rom. 14: 14, Phillips). Certainly here, too, what was important was allegiance to God and to His will.

The serpent (3: 1). Satan used the snake. It seems there was some correspondence between its shrewd ("crafty") character and his. Certainly the continued identification of Satan as "that old serpent" is significant (cf. Jn. 8: 44; Rom. 16: 20; II Cor. 11: 3; I Tim. 2: 14; Rev. 12: 9; 20: 2), as is the fact that the serpent who was used also suf-

64

fered judgment, apparently for his cooperation in the confrontation. However, if there is deeper meaning in the scene, it is obscure.

Authority (3: 16). Along with added difficulty in childbirth, the woman was told that her husband "shall rule over you." Here the theme of authority and subjection is introduced, but only after the fall. As long as Adam and Eve lived in harmony with God, harmony with one another was assured. But with sin the harmony of the natural order was destroyed. Each of us now must live under the rule of others. Only when patterns of authority exist can societies or families live healthful lives.

Work (3: 17-19). The added curse of toil placed on Adam was not the introduction of work to replace a previous blissful idleness (2: 15). But work became struggle rather than joy; a challenge to tear a living from resisting soil, replacing the creative labors in the fruit-filled Eden.

To dust (3: 19). With spiritual death, the moment the pair chose to disobey, came an initiation of the processes of physical death. Decay entered the universe. From that point in time the bodies of all men were doomed to return to their constituent elements.

The tree of life (3: 22-25). Expulsion from the garden is best seen as a gift. Only tragedy could be in store for those who now knew the living death sin brought. How awful if Adam and Eve had been doomed to live forever, to witness death's despair over and over again in each new generation. For Adam and for Eve—and for us as well—dying comes as gain, a welcome pause before resurrection launches us into life eternal.

Cain's offering (4: 2-5). Hebrews 11: 4 points out that "by faith" Abel's sacrifice was "more excellent." In Scripture, faith involves response to God's revelation. Certainly the principle of sacrifice had been demonstrated to Adam and Eve in their first clothing made of skins. It's likely the boys were so instructed by their parents or by God. Yet, only Abel brought lambs. Cain brought farm produce. It may have been the best he had, but redemption knows no acceptable sacrifice except blood. Cain's underlying attitude toward God is shown by his reaction. He was very angry. Even God's gentle urgings (4:6, 7) left him untouched.

Cain's wife (4: 17). The question is mocking and ages old. Where did Cain get his wife? A little reading gives the answer: Adam and Eve had many sons and daughters (Gen. 5: 4).

Marked for life (4: 16). Cain's punishment involved expulsion from his agricultural life and from God's own society (apparently the boys had known God and been instructed by Him, 4: 14)! A mark identified Cain, and his continued existence served as a vivid reminder to that generation of the result of rejecting God.

And so the brief report concludes with an onward glance toward future generations (4: 18-26). The seed of sin planted by Adam and Eve had sprouted in their sons, and each succeeding generation would bear bitter fruit.

As well we know.

For you and I recognize the taste of that fruit in our mouths to this very day.

GOING DEEPER

to personalize

1. Write a letter "to my children" from Adam or Eve. What might you most want to say? How would you feel? Build on the Biblical text and your own imagination, and make it real.

2. List as many personal applications of each of the following themes as you can, drawing your insights from these two chapters: (a) the root of our personal problems in the death principle, (b) Satan's model for the temptation of man, (c) rejection of personal responsibility for our sin, and/or (d) the results of sin in our relationships with others.

3. From this chapter develop a thorough definition of sin. Include a discussion of its nature, expression, results and cure.

to probe

1. Using a concordance, locate the different Hebrew and Greek words for "sin," and study at least one of them in its every appearance in the Bible. What does this tell you about yourself? What does it show you about the particular way in which you need Christ in your life?

2. Read two or three commentaries to find out their view of the nature of the first sin. If you are

interested in some particularly "heavy" study, look at commentaries discussing Romans 5: 12-21.

3. Of any book in the Bible, Romans gives perhaps the most exhaustive look at man as sinner. Read through Romans, underlining all you find concerning the nature, expression and results of sin. Then correlate these finds with Genesis 3 and 4.

A MORAL UNIVERSE

THE FIRST MEANING OF "moral" listed in the massive *The Random House Dictionary of the English Language* is: "pertaining to, or concerned with right conduct or the distinction between right and wrong." To many it is presumptuous, or even ridiculous, to suggest that we live in a moral universe. A universe, concerned with right and wrong?

But we've seen in the first chapter of Genesis that the foundation of our universe lies far back beyond nonliving matter. Certainly inert rock has no concern with right conduct. But a personal Being may!

In the creation of man (Gen. 2) there is a reflection of God's image, an image involving ability to distinguish between good and evil, and the freedom to choose. In chapters 3 and 4 we have seen the drastic consequences of man's choice to disobey God.

69

What Genesis has told us of man in God's universe is that there are certain basic, underlying realities with which we must come to grips.

Life.

Death.

Sin.

And now, in the story of the Genesis Flood, we are introduced to the twin themes of judgment and salvation. In these chapters is the proof that ours is a moral universe. God, who created and sustains it all, truly *is* concerned with right and wrong.

JUDGMENT COMING

Genesis 5 sets the scene. The genealogies do not tell us the years between Adam and the Flood. Remembering the characteristics of Hebrew genealogies (compression), we can be sure only that centuries passed, and Adam's children did begin to "multiply, and fill the earth and subdue it" (1: 28). But the taint of sin and its deadly stamp on the human personality are all too clear. Genesis 6: 5 says that "the Lord saw that the wickedness of man was great in the earth, and that every imagination of the thoughts of his heart was only evil continually." The life-style incipient in Cain, and seen in later generations in Lamech (4: 19-24), now permeated the race. Perhaps in the New Testament Book of Romans, in a passage that summarizes a decline we can trace in every civilization, we have a picture of the days of Noah as well.

Although they knew God, they neither glorified him as God nor gave thanks to him, but their thinking became futile and their foolish hearts were darkened. Although they claimed to be wise, they became fools and exchanged the glory of the immortal God for images made to look like mortal man and birds and animals and reptiles.

Therefore God gave them over in the sinful desires of their hearts to sexual impurity for the degrading of their bodies with one another. They exchanged the truth of God for a lie, and worshiped and served created things rather than the Creator—who is forever praised. . . .

Furthermore, since they did not think it worthwhile to retain the knowledge of God, he gave them over to a depraved mind, to do what ought not to be done. They have become filled with every kind of wickedness, evil, greed and depravity. They are full of envy, murder, strife, deceit and malice. They are gossips, slanderers, God-haters, insolent, arrogant and boastful; they invent ways of doing evil; they disobey their parents; they are senseless, faithless, heartless, ruthless. Although they know God's righteous decree that those who do such things deserve death, they not only continue to do these very things, but also approve of those who practice them.

Romans 1: 21-32 (NIV)

Every imagination of the thoughts of their hearts, Genesis records, was only evil continually.

The Living Bible notes, "When the Lord God saw the extent of human wickedness . . . he was sorry he had made them. It broke his heart" (Gen. 6: 5, 6). God was not unmoved. He was concerned with righteousness, and with man.

The text goes on to tell how one man in this corrupt society, Noah, walked with God. God warned Noah of coming judgment and instructed him to build a great ark: a boat in which his family and animal life might be preserved. Noah and his sons labored to complete the task, finally caulking the mighty hull with bitumen and storing fodder for the animals. Then they waited.

The Bible tells us how representatives from the animal world, "according to their kinds," found their way to the ark. When they and the human family were safely inside, the Lord sealed the door (7: 16).

The Genesis account says that in the Flood every person and animal on earth "in whose nostrils was the breath of life" died (7: 22). The New Testament puts it even stronger: "The world of that time was deluged and destroyed" (II Pet. 3: 6, NIV). Certainly the Genesis account indicates that more than a generation of mankind perished. A world that differed in significant ways from ours also was washed away. When Noah landed and finally left the ark on Mount Ararat, it was to enter a new, fresh world, a world in which the pattern of man's life and his responsibilities would change.

Long lives for men before a flood (Gen. 5) are an element of many ancient legends. The Sumerian king list gives the length of the reign of one pre-flood ruler as extending up to 43,200 years! This reflects traditions both of a flood and extended life before its deluge. Also, before the Biblical Flood, men were apparently vegetarian. Now God gives Noah flesh to eat. Now, too, human government is instituted as the responsibility of man to govern man. Capital punishment is commanded for murder because it is the ultimate denial of the worth and value of human life. So Noah is set down in a new world where he is to learn a new way of life.

As Noah was deposited in a new world to learn a new life-style, so the believer is brought into a totally new experience in Christ, "not [to] live the rest of his earthly life for evil human desires, but rather for the will of God" (cf. I Pet. 3: 20—4: 11, NIV). Judgment does strike down man because of sin, yet with the judgment, escape is provided for those who look to God in faith.

In the waters of the Flood, then, we see God speak out in affirmation and in warning. This *is* a moral universe. God *is* concerned about right and wrong, and God will act to punish wrong. Peter sums up the message of the Flood in these words:

In the last days scoffers will come, scoffing and following their own evil desires. They will say, "Where is this 'coming' he promised? Ever since our fathers died, everything goes on as it has since the beginning of creation." But they deliberately forget that long ago by God's word the heavens existed and the earth was formed out of water and with water. By water also the world of that time was deluged and destroyed. By the same word the present heavens and earth are reserved for fire, being kept for the day of judgment and destruction of ungodly men. . . . But the day of the Lord will come like a thief. The heavens will disappear with a roar; the elements will be destroyed by fire, and the earth and everything in it will be laid bare.

II Peter 3: 3-7, 10 (NIV)

In the destruction of that day, when what is solid now dissolves, and things now unseen remain, the moral nature of the universe will be fully known. God, who in the Flood etched His moral message indelibly on our world, will expose even those who cover their eyes to the final moral reality.

DID THE FLOOD HAPPEN?

Many are willing to accept the Genesis Flood story as a myth revealing essential religious truth. But they draw back from any claim of historicity. And many conservatives who believe that a flood really did happen argue for a limited flood—a flood of local rather than worldwide extent. They point out that God's purpose was to judge the race of man, suggesting that probably mankind had not as yet spread beyond the Fertile Crescent Valley.

Behind this line of argument lies the almost universally accepted view of scientific uniformitarianism. This is the theory that all that we find in our world biologically and particularly geologically, can be explained by processes which presently operate in the physical universe. Geologic uniformitarianism, which suggests that millenniums of erosion and repeated ice ages sculptured earth's topography, is accepted and taught in many Christian colleges. While these Christian scientists unhesitatingly accept the creationist view of life and the special creative act by which God made man, they do not take seriously the view that once our earth knew a universal flood.

Uniformitarianism, the view that "everything goes on as it has since the beginning of creation" (II Pet. 3: 4, NIV), maintains its sway.

Universal? The term "universal" presents two distinct questions to the believer. Does the Biblical account of the Flood necessarily teach that it was worldwide? And, if the Bible does indicate a universal Flood, is the geologic record so sure that we must question the accuracy of Genesis?

Many have argued that Genesis must be understood to describe a universal Flood. They point to the following evidence:

■ Every living thing was to be destroyed in the Flood waters (7: 4). This assumes that man and animal life had spread in the centuries or the millenniums since the fall far beyond the Mesopotamian Plain.

■ After the Flood God specifically states that "every living thing" was in fact destroyed (8: 21, NASB).

■ The text states clearly that "all the high mountains under the whole heaven were covered" to a depth of at least 23 feet [15 cubits] (7: 19).

■ Finally, the ark is said to have come to rest "upon the mountains of Ararat," a range that reaches some 10,000 feet in height (8: 4). A local Flood might have brought them to the foothills. But "upon" the mountains?

This textual argument has been answered by suggesting that "all the high mountains" refers simply to all the heights in the inhabited area. And that "the whole heaven" is phenomenological language, that is, it refers to the visible heavens so far as Noah and his culture were concerned, or to the horizon. To support this view, Driver and others computed the amount of water required to cover the mountains and argued that not nearly enough exists within our seas and atmosphere. But this in turn rests on the uniformitarian assumption. Was the pre-Flood world essentially like ours geologically and geographically? Or is it possible that the mountain heights and the sea depths we know were in fact caused by the watery cataclysm of the Flood?

Cataclysm. Recently Christians and non-Christians have suggested that geologic features of our earth must be explained in terms of one or more past cataclysms. Detailed scientific arguments have been advanced, pointing out data not readily explained on the uniformitarian hypothesis. As a popularizing laymen has asked:

> Why were dinosaurs quickly drowned and buried in sediments? Why were mammoths quickly drowned in North America, and quick frozen or flash frozen in Siberia, even with sub-tropical vegetation in their mouths and stomachs? Why were petrified forests found one hundred miles from the South pole by Admiral Byrd? Why were land mammals found fossilized in locations below sea level, and why were sea animals found fossilized at high elevations?[1]

The same author tells of a tree found in an English quarry "about one hundred feet long, and at a forty degree angle. It went through strata after strata, each supposedly laid down millions of years apart. At the top the tree was about one foot in diameter. At the bottom it was five feet in one radius and two feet in the other radius, as if it had come under immense pressure."

In a controversial 1961 book,[2] Dr. Henry M. Morris, a hydrolics engineer, and Dr. John C. Whitcomb, an Old Testament professor, thoroughly explored the geologic and fossil evidence

---

1. Donald W. Patten, "The Noachian Flood and Mountain Uplift," in *Creation*, Henry M. Morris, ed. (Grand Rapids: Baker, 1968), p. 102.

2. Henry M. Morris and John C. Whitcomb, *The Genesis Flood* (Grand Rapids: Baker, 1961).

and attempted to demonstrate that a Flood geology better explains the physical data. Their picture suggests a pre-Flood world insulated by great concentrations of water vapor in the atmosphere (partially explaining the lengthened life as due to blockage of cosmic radiation, which has been shown to be associated with aging). The Flood itself involved not only the release of this mass to fall on earth, but also the breaking up of "fountains of the great deep" (7: 11), subterranean waters beneath a flat and shallow single continent. This unimaginable hydrologic power and weight broke up the land mass (causing what science now recognizes as the puzzling "continental drift"), and also caused the depression of the ocean beds and the upthrust of the mountain ranges that mark the earth of our time.

A later, similar cataclysmic view postulates the approach to earth of a giant comet or another planet. This celestial catastrophe, with the fantastic gravitational interactions involved, would cause tides of subcontinental dimensions, with the earth's lava itself flowing and heaving and land masses jolted out of shape. Many of the unexplainable features of fossil and rock records would find a ready explanation.

The point of all this, of course, is not that evidence exists to compel acceptance of the universal Flood theory. The point is simply this: There is no necessary reason to base our interpretation of the Scriptures on current geological theory. The Flood may have been local. On the other hand, the

Flood may have been the single greatest shaper of the features of the world we now know. But whichever happened in the past, we can be confident that as we read the Genesis text we are revisiting history, and that in the account of these events we do meet God and hear His message.

We do live in a moral universe.

Sin brings judgment, for the God behind it all cares about right and wrong.

Yet we see that He still cares for us as well. The surging waters of judgment may swirl around you and me. But God has prepared an ark. Through faith in His Son, like Noah, you and I can be carried safely through to Christ's new world.

OBSERVATIONS ON THE TEXT

As in other early Genesis chapters, many things here draw our attention and stimulate our curiosity. Most of them we can only speculate about. Yet it is fascinating to observe them.

The sons of God (6: 2). Were these fallen angels (cf. Job 1: 6) who somehow impregnated human women and fathered Nephilim (giants as it says in the King James)? Were they the sons of princes as rabbinic tradition holds? Or was there an intermingling of the "godly" line of Seth with that of Cain?

The word Nephilim is used in only two places in the Bible, and it is not at all certain it means "giant." A different word is used when giants like Goliath are referred to. If this problem arouses your curiosity, use an analytical concordance and several commentaries on Genesis to throw more light on the different interpretations.

Change of heart (6: 7). Does God's sorrow at man's descent into deeper expression of sin show regret for Creation? Is this His confession of a mistake? How are we to understand God's expression of anguish and regret?

The ark's size (6: 15-17). Using the smallest known size for the cubit (18 inches rather than 22 inches), the ark was built with three decks, about 450 feet long, 75 feet wide and 45 feet in height, displacing some 43,000 tons. Thus it had the proportion and size of some modern oceangoing vessels.

The animal "kinds" (6: 20). In the past, "kinds" sometimes has been translated "species," a term now used in many different senses in biology. It is likely that the many breeds of dogs, for instance, were represented in a single pair. Also, note that seven pairs of "clean" (that is, sacrificial and food animals) were taken into the ark, and probably so used after the waters receded.

Length of the Flood. The following chart, adapted from Pfeiffer,[3] traces the events of the Flood.

Promise (8: 21, 22). The uniformitarian principle is introduced here, after the Flood, as promised. God will not again interrupt the regular flow of seasons or break into the orderly actions of natural law to judge the race.

3. Charles F. Pfeiffer, *Introduction to the Old Testament* (New York: Harper & Row, 1941), p. 32.

FIGURE III   **EVENTS OF THE FLOOD**

Month	Day	Events	Number of Days
8	27	Waters settle 15 cubits	34
10	1	Ark on dry ground. Noah waits.	40
11	11	Noah sends raven, waits.	7
11	18	Noah sends dove, waits.	7
11	25	Dove sent again, returns with olive leaf. Noah waits.	7
12	2	Noah again sends dove, no return. Noah continues to wait.	29
1	1	Noah removes covering. No water seen. Noah waits.	56
2	27	God commands them to leave the ark. Total time of Flood.	370

Rainbow (8: 12-17). Why was the rainbow selected as the sign of the covenant promise between God and mankind? Could it have been because it only appeared after the Flood, due to drastically changed atmospheric conditions caused by the dropping of the water canopy? It's fascinating to suppose that when he left the ark Noah saw the beauty of the rainbow for the first time in his 600 years.

Canaan's curse (9: 18-28). The meaning of "saw the nakedness of his father" (9: 22) is obscure. But the clear implications of the picture of the drunken Noah and the moral fault in Ham make one thing clear. Men may have been significantly changed. But man's heritage from Adam—his sin nature—remained.

81

Many have noted that the "curse" on Canaan is in fact a prophetic utterance by Noah. His words are not the cause of what would later happen, but foretell it. It is important to note that only Canaan of the Hametic family was selected out. The peoples involved are not the Negroid, but the peoples who later inhabited the land of Canaan (Palestine) before the Israelites.

The table of nations (Gen. 10). Of the 70 names selected for inclusion in this list some are well known to Bible scholars and students of ancient history (as "Mizraim," Egypt). Others are lost in antiquity. And still other peoples, like the Sumerians, are not included at all.

Babel (Gen. 11). The "fresh start" given Noah's clan soon settled into sin's stagnation. Told to go out and replenish the earth (9: 1), Noah's descendants settled on a single plain, "Lest we be scattered abroad upon the face of the whole earth" (11: 4). They built a tower, which probably resembled the Babylonian ziggurat, possibly for astrological divination or perhaps even in the hope that its top "in the heavens" would provide a place of refuge should another flood come.

In any case, this disobedience led the Lord to act in a fresh judgment. He confused the languages. If you ever doubt God's sense of humor, picture sometime the next morning when one of the workers asked another for a brick!

These peoples refused to go out and fulfill God's plan. So now He "scattered them abroad . . . over the face of all the earth" (11: 8).

And so we come to an end of the first act of the cosmic drama. Up to this time God has dealt with the whole human race. And mankind has demonstrated in each response the distortion of the original image which sin brings. Yet, in it all, there are glimmerings of hope. God speaks, and some respond with faith. So now the Scriptures focus on the men who do believe. In the genealogy of chapter 11 we are prepared for our introduction to one man, Abram, on whose faith the future of the race of man depends.

GOING DEEPER

to personalize

1. Study II Peter 3: 3-18 to determine how you and I are to apply the Flood story to our own lives.

2. Write briefly, summarizing Genesis 1-9 to give a picture of man in God's universe. How basic do you think these chapters are to the development of a Biblical world view?

to probe

There are many areas of Genesis 6-9 that stimulate us to do research. Using tools such as books on Old Testament archaeology, commentaries, books and articles on the Flood, etc., write your own brief documented answer to at least one of the following questions:

1. Outline the different positions on who the Nephilim were. Which do you prefer? Why?

2. What did the ark look like?

3. Genesis 9: 6 indicates capital punishment. What else does the Bible say on this subject?

4. Does the suggestion of God "repenting" indicate that He regrets an earlier mistake?

5. What is the relationship between the tower of Babel and the ziggurat?

6. How does the epic of Gilgamesh parallel and differ from the Biblical Flood story?

7. What is some of the evidence Flood geologists claim cannot be explained by uniformitarianism?

8. On what basis do uniformitarians reject the views of the catastrophists?

9. How does the book *Worlds in Collision,* by Immanuel Velikovsky (Dell paperback), a non-Christian, relate to Biblical catastrophism?

THE SUFFERER

HISTORY IS OFTEN SO IMPERSONAL. The great events are drawn in with a heavy pen, the sweeping movements that affect nations carefully recorded. But all too often the ordinary man is unmentioned. We see the armies march but fail to enter the hut of the peasant.

While the Bible is history, it is not impersonal history. We're invited in Scripture to share the experiences of men and women like ourselves and to enter into their struggles to relate the great Personality behind the universe to themselves.

PROLOGUE

Job 1: 1–2: 10

When we meet Job we're immediately impressed. He was a surprisingly pious man, and a very wealthy one. As was common in those days, Job served as family priest. We note that his material wealth hadn't led him to pride, but seemed to have deepened his sense of humility and his awareness of sin. In fact, he regularly offered sacrifices to God to cover possible hidden sins of his family! Job knew of nothing against his sons, but he also knew the deceit of the human heart and therefore followed the example of Abel rather than that of Cain.

Our own impression of Job finds surprising corroboration. While we're visiting this man, God Himself is pointing Job out to Satan.

Job 1: 6-12 depicts a striking scene. Satan presents himself to God and makes his report (1: 6, 7). At this particular time God directs Satan's attention to Job. "There is none like him," the Lord comments, "a blameless and upright man, who fears God and turns away from evil."

Satan responds to suggest that Job's piety is certainly profitable! "Haven't you put a hedge about him on every side?" Then Satan proposes a test. If God will only *take away* the blessings Job has been given, Satan says, "he will curse thee to thy face" (1: 11). And so the ground rules for the test are laid. God is to permit Satan to attack the protected believer, and Satan is to force from Job's tortured lips a rejection of the Lord!

What happens then is too familiar. In a single day all that Job has is torn from him. His cattle are rustled by Sabeans, and his herders killed. His sheep are destroyed by fire falling from Heaven. His camels are lost to a raid by the Chaldeans.

And a tornado strikes the house where his ten children are feasting, and all the young people are killed. And the Bible tells us, "Then Job arose, and rent his robe, and shaved his head [signs of mourning in the East], and fell upon the ground, and worshiped" (1: 20). Total tragedy had not torn a denial of God from Job's lips, nor did his anguish lead him to charge God with wrong.

But Satan was not done. When on another day God points out that Job "holds fast his integrity" (2: 3), Satan cynically asks for the ultimate test. "All that a man has he will give for his life" (2: 4). So God permits Satan to touch Job's person. For any extremity short of death, Job is delivered to the tempter's power.

The extremity of the physical suffering is hard for us to imagine now. But we have a witness. Job's wife is finally moved to beg Job to "curse God, and die" (2: 9), and so find death's release. But Job responds, "Shall we receive good at the hand of God, and shall we not receive evil?" To Job the Lord is still God. So Satan meets his defeat. "In all this Job did not sin with his lips" (2: 10).

This is the last time we meet Satan in the Book of Job. The initial test is over. But Job's suffering does not end. In fact, Job's suffering seems to continue. We have to conclude that there is more involved here than a personal battle between God and Satan, with Job as a hapless pawn.

In fact the Book of Job can perhaps be best understood if we see it as a cosmic court scene where Job has his sincerity and integrity questioned by

Satan, the "prosecuting attorney," then finds his friends acting as witnesses against him. God acts as judge and finally vindicates Job. The tension revolves around the question of why the righteous suffer, and moves the discussion naturally into considering the nature of God. And so we enter, with Job, into a painful struggle to understand.

THE THREE FRIENDS

Outwardly unmoved, inwardly Job was in turmoil. As the days of agony continued, the inner doubts and fears were far more excruciating for Job than the physical pain. Here was a man who had built his life on piety and honesty. Now the God he served had turned against him. Certainly the timing and method of the losses Job suffered made it clear: this was the hand of the Lord.

The question that tormented Job was "Why?" When three friends came from their cities to comfort and console Job, they could hardly recognize him. In tears, they sat with him for seven days and nights, so moved by his suffering that they could not bring themselves to speak. Then, plagued by the tormenting questions within, Job began the dialogue that continues through the next 28 chapters of the book that bears his name. We can summarize and modernize the language and trace the lines of argument as these four men struggle with the problem of suffering and evil in human experience. These are men like you and me, who feel the heat of suffering's flame and are desperate to at least understand what they cannot avoid.

In the dialogue we'll hear their thoughts and fears. And, perhaps, in this and the next study on Job (chap. 7), we'll gain something more. Something Job himself needed: A deeper knowledge of God.

Job 3: 1-26.

"I'm sorry I was ever born. Why didn't I die at birth? I'd have been better off. At least there's no misery then.

"I knew things were going too good. I was afraid of something like this all along.

"I'd be better off dead than suffering all this trouble."

Eliphaz (4: 1–5: 27).

"I've got to answer that. Remember how you counseled other people? Remember how you held out hope to those who would walk in integrity?

"After all, the innocent don't perish. God punishes the sinner. If I were you, I'd turn to God.

"God is clearly chastising you, and when you turn to Him, He'll restore you."

Job (6: 1–7: 21).

"If you only knew how much God is making me suffer! I wish He'd crush me and get it over with!

"As for you, Eliphaz, you're a lot of help. Show me what I've done wrong! I tell you the truth: I just can't be suffering a chastisement. I've been good. . . .

"Oh, how I'm suffering! I just can't keep quiet any longer. I tell you, I'm terrified! I'd rather die in a minute.

"Why does God let this happen? If I'd sinned He could have pardoned it. What's happening to me?"

Bildad (8: 1-22).

"That's a terrible way to talk! Is God ever unjust? Never!

"If you were pure and prayed to God, He'd surely pardon you.

"Just think back. Our fathers taught us that the man who forgets God is the one who fails. But God doesn't punish the upright. So you're bound to come out all right [aside] if you're upright."

Job (9: 1–10: 22).

"I know what you're saying is true. But how can anyone really have any standing with God? He's so far above us. What can I say to Him? How can I reach Him? . . .

"I wish I could. I wish I could plead my innocence in some court. But who's going to judge between me and God? I say I'm righteous, but God still afflicts me.

"And no one can judge, can make Him stop whipping me.

"I wish I could die.

"God, cut it out!

"I didn't do anything. Show me where I sinned. You know I'm not wicked.

"If I were, I'd deserve punishment. But I don't. Why did you ever let me grow up to be mistreated like this, and then just to die?"

Zophar (11: 1-20).

"How can you expect to be justified talking like that?

"Why, you're full of boasting!

" 'I'm just,' you say. 'I'm pure,' you blab.

"Ha! If God would talk, He'd tell you! God knows. He sees secret sin.

"But there's still hope. Get your heart right with God, and He'll still accept you. But watch out. There's no escape for the wicked. Their only hope is death."

Job (12: 1–14: 22).

"You guys are so smart. You sure know it all!

"Well, I know just as much as you do.

"I know God has all wisdom and power.

"I know He sets people up, and knocks them down. Sure God is working in our lives. . . .

"Oh, I wish I could talk to God about it. You stick up for God, and say I must be wrong.

"Well, you're wrong! You're unfair, on His side.

"I know I'm right. I'd say it to God's face as well as to yours. I'm right. I haven't done wrong.

"O God, it's not fair! Men are so frail. So weak. Stop it! Don't do this to me. You're wearing away all my hope."

Eliphaz (15: 1-35).

"Job, you've been rambling on like a fool. Why, that kind of talk itself condemns you.

"You don't know everything. God is wiser than you.

"Remember what we know about God.

"It is the wicked man who suffers.

"It is the proud man God brings low—the man who boasts against God.

"It's the godless who suffer in the end."

Job (16: 1–17: 16).

"Oh, you're a miserable bunch of comforters.

"Whether I talk like this or keep quiet, I still suffer.

"The fact is, God's against me. He's delivered me to the ungodly. He's putting unbearable pressure on me.

"Scoff if you will. But let heaven and earth be my witness. It's not happening because of my guilt.

"People spit on me. They mock me. You mock me with your arguments.

"My only hope is to die. Let my moldering body find rest as dust."

Bildad (18: 1-21).

"Why keep on trying to justify yourself? We all know it's the wicked man who suffers terrors and who falls into calamity.

"And, oh, the wicked will suffer!

"Their families will die—no one will carry on the family name.

"The wicked will dash in terror toward death. Surely this is the horrible fate of the man who doesn't know God."

Job (19: 1-29).

"Stop it! Stop it! I'm not wicked. Oh, for justice—just simple justice.

"But there's no hope. God's crushed me. Even you, even my relatives, have turned against me.

"Everyone says, 'God is punishing Job.' Have pity, friends. Have pity. Why do you persecute me like God does?

"I wish my side were published. Someone would vindicate me. But you—you're afraid to take my side!"

Zophar (20: 1-29).

"That's enough!

"Don't you know that ever since men have been on earth that the wicked only get away with sin for a time?

"They might seem to prosper, but in the end the wicked man's life is one of gall and bitterness. His possessions will be gone, his children dead. He won't keep on prospering. God will unleash all the fierceness of His wrath on him.

"That's what always happens to the wicked man.

"Get that, Job? To the wicked man!"

Job (21: 1-34).

"Listen. Listen, and then mock. But now listen, and be surprised.

"You talk about the end of the wicked. Well, look around. We each know wicked men who do prosper. They get old. They see their grandchildren. Their houses are safe, nothing bad seems to happen to them.

"God doesn't use His rod on them. Why, they mock God! They say, 'Why serve God? We're doing all right without Him. Where's the profit in prayer?'

"How often do folks like this really get what they deserve?

"Oh, you say, they get it in the end.

"But *when?* Why, God's children seem to suffer more than the ungodly!

"*Who* repays the wicked? Your answers are all lies!"

Eliphaz (22: 1-30).

"Well, what good is it to God that you're so righteous? Do you suppose He's clapping and jumping up and down over your goodness?

"Why does He reprove you, then?

"Let's face it. This has happened because you're a big, wicked, terrible sinner!

"God knows. He sees things we didn't, things ou ε done at night, skulking around.

"But now you've showed your true colors. Who said, 'What's the profit in prayer?' Why, that's your own heart talking. You hypocrite!

"Listen, Job, seek God now. Listen to Him. If you return to God and put away your sins, He'll restore all the good things you had.

"Pray. God will hear you.

"God saves the humble man, the innocent. Turn from your sin. You can still be delivered."

Job (23: 1–24: 25).

"I wish I could talk to God. He'd have to listen. I'm right. I am innocent. God would have to agree.

"But He's hidden—He's hiding.

"I've done right.

"I've done His will.

"I've kept His commandments.

"Why does He do this to me? I'm terrified! . . .

"God knows what's happening, but He doesn't act. People are murdered. People steal. People commit adultery. And the poor suffer.

"And the wicked prosper! God upholds them. Be honest. It's true.

"Prove me a liar."

Bildad (25: 1-6).

"God is always right. We men, how can we be

95

just with God? How could we, worms that we are, explain His actions?"

Job (26: 1–27: 12).

"How you've helped poor weak me. Thanks!

"I know God's power—His majesty. How far beyond our conception His might is.

"But as God lives, He's treating me unjustly.

"I won't lie, even for God.

"I won't confess sin.

"I have been righteous. I'll hold to that fact as long as I live.

"I'll never admit it's my fault."

Zophar (27: 13–28: 28).[1]

"I say it again. God does indeed judge the wicked.

"Wealth is hidden in a mine, deep underground, out of sight. But it's there. God's ways aren't to be compared with wealth—sapphires, gold, rubies—for value. But God's wisdom may be as hard to seek out.

"But remember, Job. He is God! As for us, it is enough to know that 'the fear of the Lord is wisdom, to leave evil is understanding.' "

---

1. The speeches up to this point have come in regular cycles. Here, however, it would appear that for some reason Zophar's third speech is missing. However, Job 27: 13 is very similar to the end of Zophar's last speech in 20: 29, and it is reasonable to attribute this following section to him, or to suppose that Job is himself giving a parody of Zophar's position.

Job (29: 1–31: 40)

"I've never done any wrong. If I have, convict me. I'll take my punishment.
"But I haven't.
"I am clean.
"That's all I have to say."

GOING DEEPER

to personalize and to probe

Focus attention now on the dialogue segment covering Job 2—31. Examine it carefully (using the summarized dialogue or going to the extended Bible text if you wish) and respond to the following:

1. Summarize in a series of statements Job's understanding of his situation.

2. Summarize in a series of statements Job's friends' understanding of his situation.

3. Read the whole dialogue again and jot down a word describing the dominant feeling communicated by each speaker in each speech.

4. The dialogue focuses on exploring the reason for suffering. What explanation do the three friends have for suffering? Why can't Job accept their explanation for his case? What explanation does Job have for his suffering?

5. Why do you think the three friends reacted so strongly to Job's speeches from 21: 1 on? Does it demand more faith or less faith to look at evidence that seems to challenge your faith? Why?

THE MESSAGE OF JOB

IN MANY WAYS the Book of Job is disquieting. Largely, perhaps, because we're introduced here to God as mystery. And mystery is something that, throughout the ages, people have felt driven to explain.

Barbara's brother was killed in an accident when both were 19. The answer of her pastor, "Barbara, it was just an accident. God is good, and He couldn't have planned anything like that," failed to satisfy her. The death set Barbara on a five-year search for an answer, in the course of which she met Jesus Christ as personal Savior. But she still has no answer for "Why?"

Paul Kahle's brother trained for nearly a decade to become a Missionary Aviation Fellowship pilot. He crashed during his first month of service in West Irian and was killed. Paul, who knows that God is good *and* that God is in charge, also felt compelled to ask the unanswerable.

99

As long as "Why?" is posed as a general question, we can find answers. Why did God permit sin? To be "in God's image" man had to be truly free. Why does our civilization know death and brutality, war and crime? Because death is in our veins. God's image may be the source of good. But we bear Adam's likeness as well. Spiritually dead, our personalities are warped by selfishness, by surging emotion, by a captive will. From the Hitlers of history to the "little" sins that mark our own lives, we see death's decay.

While the general questions have answers we can accept, the specific questions about our own personal experience often do not. "Why have I been so lonely?" "Why is my husband an alcoholic?" "Why have my children dropped out of school?" "Why did that automobile accident kill my mother?" "Why should *I* have cancer?" "Lord, why me?"

Somehow life brings each of us to crisis, driving each of us to ask Job's question. Hoping against hope that understanding will bring relief from our uncertainty, or perhaps even show us what we can do to move a suddenly implacable God, we plunge into our own agonized exploration of mystery.

We feel so comfortable with a God we fully understand, a God who operated, computer-like, by clear and unbreakable rules. But often the motives of God are far beyond our power to penetrate.

It is this kind of personal pressure that the Book of Job describes. The accepted truths about God that Job and his three friends relied on seem now to break down. God confronts them as mystery and only Job dares face the challenge of examining the assumptions on which his life has been built.

GOD AND MORALITY

The Book of Job helps us see that men had knowledge of God even before written revelation. It was imperfect knowledge. But there was witness enough for the response of faith.

The dialogue of Job recognizes God as transcendent. Here is no pagan "nature God," a personification of some created thing like the sun or moon or beast or man. This God, so far above creation, cannot be contacted by man's initiative. Still, He interests Himself in man's affairs. In fact, God's holy character is expressed in active supervision of the lives of men. As a moral Judge, God intervenes to punish the sinner and to bless the righteous. A good man can expect good from His hand; an evil man can expect punishment. Of course, men are frail. Despite every good intention, men still sin. And so there is recognition of the need for sacrifice and repentance and prayer. These will reestablish a man with God again, for the Lord is forgiving.

Such ideas about God are in harmony with the written revelation of our Bible. We can hardly fault these men for their basic concept of God. Their God-concept is, in fact, a clear testimony that God continued to give witness to Himself to all men through history and tradition.

It's also striking to look at Job's last speech and note the morality it shows. Job, in chapters 29-31, describes the principles of right and wrong according to which he has lived. When Job served as a judge, seated with other elders at the city gates, he "delivered the poor who cried, and the fatherless who had none to help him" (29: 12). He searched out any who were defrauded or taking advantage of the poor or disabled, to break "the fangs of the unrighteous, and made him drop his prey" (29: 17). Job took an active role in crusading for what we call social justice today. In our modern world he would have been an aggressive enemy of city slum landlords and economic theft. So Job sat proudly among men, respected for his honesty and concern for the needy as well as known for his wealth.

Job's sexual life was pure also. His public and private morality matched. He did not lust after the virgins or envy his neighbor's wife (31: 1, 9). Job rejected falsehood and dealt honestly with all. No thumb on the scales for Job; what he sold he always weighed out fairly, giving full measure. If any of his employees had a complaint, Job listened to them and never "rejected the cause" (31: 13). (If only management and labor had this attitude today!)

If any poor had need, if any strangers were hungry, if any were perishing from lack of clothing, Job met their need. Although rich, Job avoided the great hazard of the materialist. He put his confidence in God, not in his wealth. He even avoided prideful joy in his riches. Never was Job false to God by lifting possessions or idols above the Lord.

No wonder the Scriptures tell us God pointed Job out to Satan as a unique servant, and affirmed, "There is none like him on the earth, a blameless and upright man, who fears God and turns away from evil" (2: 3). Job was a truly admirable man.

Yet it was to a man like this that the divine judgment seemed to come. In Job's case, it was not an evil man who suffered at the Lord's hand, but a good man. In the face of this mystery, Job and his friends were forced to examine the foundations of their faith and to question the very concept they had of God.

And this is what the Book of Job asks us to do: To risk confronting mystery. To be willing to admit that perhaps the idea we have of God may not be God at all!

ELIHU'S CONTRIBUTION

The Book of Job is organized in a clear way to carry on the exploration of mystery and then bring us to an amazing conclusion.

The book opens with a prologue. Here we see Job's integrity questioned. God permits Satan to attack Job, an attempt to make this man reject the Lord. But Job stands firm and will not reject God.

In the second section of the book we are drawn into a dialogue between Job and three friends who struggle to explain the mystery. The three friends hold fast to their brittle concept of God, sure that God *must* act in a determined way to punish sin and reward good. Because they admit God no freedom, they conclude that Job must have sinned and God must have acted to judge and to condemn.

The tragedy of the dialogue is that Job is in essential agreement with the three! He can find no explanation but sin for suffering. Yet Job knows that he has not sinned! Impaled on the agonizing dilemma, Job feels forced to go further and further in questioning God's justice. Finally he faces a reality we're all aware of but which Job's friends apparently make a conscious effort to deny. In this world it is *not* always the unrighteous who suffer! Scoffers prosper and profit! In fact, believers may have a harder time than unbelievers!

This line of thought is fearfully rejected by the three, who redouble their attack on Job. Job must be forced to admit that he has sinned. For now it seems that if Job cannot be convicted, the picture of God they have hung in their hearts to worship will be shattered. Finally at an impass, condemned by his friends but certain of his own integrity, Job refuses to argue anymore.

Job himself is uncomfortable with his challenge to God's fairness. But he has found no resolution to the problem. If Job is not at fault, then somehow, unthinkable as it may be, Job's God must bear the blame.

```
                    OUTLINE OF JOB
    Job 1, 2            prologue
    Job 3—31           dialogue with three friends
    Job 32-37          Elihu's contribution
    Job 38—42:6        God speaks
    Job 42:7-17        epilogue
```

Elihu speaks. Now a young observer breaks in (Job 32—37). Elihu has kept silent out of respect for the age of Job and his three friends, listening as they searched for a solution to the dilemma. But as their discussion has returned again and again to the circular logic of a syllogistic understanding of God, Elihu felt about to burst (32: 19). For Elihu has, if not a solution, at least insights to share.

The first contribution Elihu makes is to break the pattern that has held Job and his friends in its cold grip. The three had insisted, "Suffering is caused by sin; Job is suffering; Job has sinned." Job rejects the conclusion but cannot reject either premise! His cry then was to assert, "God is causing me to suffer unjustly." Now Elihu suggests that punishment need not be seen as the only cause of suffering! In fact, Elihu notes, *God may use suffering to instruct as well as punish* (33: 19-30).

At this point Elihu turns to Job as well, and points out that his words also lacked knowledge and insight (34: 35). He has no solution to the problem of suffering to ascribe unrighteousness to God. "Far be it from God that he should do wick-

105

edness, and from the Almighty that he should do wrong," Elihu affirms (34: 10). We take as our starting point not our own experience or our own righteousness, but the starting point in our search must be a firm trust in the wisdom and justice of God. We may not understand God. But we can, and we must, trust Him.

These twin themes are repeated through Elihu's speech. God has purposes in suffering, such as opening men's ears to listen to Him (36: 15). God does great things. We can't even understand His ways in the physical universe. Why then should we expect to fully understand His ways with men (37: 5)?

We will never be able to "find out" God or categorize Him so that He fits in our boxes. We can only know that He is great in power and justice, and that His character is marked by an "abundant righteousness he will not violate" (37: 23).

God intervenes (Job 38–41). Elihu has prepared the way. Now God's voice is heard. God's answer to Job is unexpected. Rather than reassuring the sufferer or explaining "Why," God picks up a theme introduced by Elihu. In His first speech (38: 1—40: 2), God reveals His omnipotence. Only God entered into the springs of the seas and strode the canyons that split the ocean deeps. Only God set the stars in place and established their course. It is by God's wisdom the hawk soars; it is He who designed the eagle's far-seeing eye. Confronted with God's wisdom and omnipotence, Job is now invited to plead his case with the Lord (40: 1, 2).

Silenced, Job has nothing to say, but covers his mouth in awe (40: 4, 5).

God now carries Job on a journey toward self-insight. While the first revelation emphasized God's omnipotence, the second (40: 10—41: 34) compares God with human frailty. Man even stands impotent before creatures. Crocodile and rhino awe men and laugh at their puny weapons. How then can a man expect to stand before the One who made these awesome beasts? Job's urgent demand to meet God on equal terms, as man to man, to stand before some impartial court with jurisdiction over both, has in fact lost sight of the basic reality. The Lord is God. Job is merely man.

Job now accepts the position of a creature before the Creator.

I have uttered what I did not understand,
　　things too wonderful for me,
which I did not know . . . .

I had heard of thee by the hearing of the ear,
　　but now my eye sees thee;
therefore I despise myself,
　　and repent in dust and ashes.

Job 42: 3-6

The confrontation is over. Job has bowed his knee. Job has recognized God as God. Beyond this, the questioning sufferer has received no answer.

EPILOGUE

The conclusion to the story (42: 7-16) seems to many an anticlimax. Job's wealth is restored in double. He has seven more sons and three more daughters. And Job is told to pray for his three friends because, God says to them, "You have not spoken of me what is right, as my servant Job has" (42: 7).

Thus the Book of Job leaves us with more questions than when we began.

How did Job speak what was right, and his friends incur God's anger in the dialogue? Perhaps because only Job was willing to test his concept of God against his own experience and observation. True faith is not a retreat from reality but a willingness to face mystery. Job's three friends were unwilling to admit the possibility that their understanding of God might be imperfect. Is it possible that their trust was not in Him but in an image they had constructed in His likeness?

What is the answer to the "Why" of Job's suffering? No answer is given in the text. There are hints. For instance, at the beginning of Job's complaint he cries out that what he feared has come upon him, that what he dreaded has at last happened (3: 25). Can it be that Job's relationship with God was flawed by a fear that blocked full trust and love? Certainly Job's meeting with God replaced hearing with sight. Job lost all trust in his own righteousness as the basis for his standing with God (42: 6), and simply bowed down before the Lord.

Deep release and freedom are available for us too when we let God's perfect love cast out our fear and no longer think of what we do as having any merit in God's eyes, or meriting reward. Like Job we need to learn to rest on abandonment of any righteousness of our own, and trust instead His great affirmations of our value and worth. For isn't our relationship with God rooted in love's Calvary expression? Perhaps (and only perhaps) God's goal had always been the deepening of His personal relationship with Job.

What do we learn about our suffering? One message is clear. We wrong God if we fall into the way of thinking of the three friends. We wrong God if each trial of ours is excused by condemning ourselves for supposed sin. Instead, we need to approach God with trust in both His love and righteousness; His purposes will be just and for our good.

The New Testament adds special insight here. In I Peter God assures those who also suffer though they have done right that, should such suffering come, it reflects a special purposive act of God. Christ's suffering is given as an example of the just suffering and of the fact that through such "injustices" great good is wrought. On Calvary, Jesus' suffering brought us to God (I Pet. 3: 13-18).

So we can know this. Job's suffering also had a good purpose, a purpose for which Job had to trust God. Our suffering is purposive too, and we too must trust.

We may not see the purpose.
We may not understand.
But we can trust God.

Confronted with mystery, we are freed through a personal relationship with God to face conflict and inner turmoil honestly, and to affirm a faith in God which does not rest on the fact that we understand or know. Like Job, we're free to bow our hearts before God and trust.

GOING DEEPER

to personalize

1. Select one chapter from Elihu's discourse or one chapter from the section of God's discourse and examine it carefully. You may want to rewrite it in modern terms to express fully what the speaker says.

2. On page 108 the author lists unanswered questions and suggests possible answers. First, see if you agree with his suggestions, and then go on to suggest further ideas of your own. See if it's possible to list additional unanswered questions.

3. Study I Peter 3: 13-17. How does this help you to face difficult times in your own life? Can you contrast the response suggested in I Peter to Job's reaction to his suffering?

4. Look finally at James' comment on Job (5: 8-11). What does this tell us about the message of Job for us?

to probe

1. From the Book of Job construct a detailed theology, that is, carefully define how men of that day viewed God. What areas do you feel further revelation needed to clarify? Were there any areas in which serious distortions seem present? (Note: Remember that in reporting dialogue the doctrine of inspiration does not guarantee the truth of what speakers say. It guarantees only that the dialogue is reported accurately. For instance, Satan called God a liar. Inspiration hardly requires us to accept that statement as truth! Thus, to suggest that Job's theology is imperfect is not to cast doubt on either the inspiration or authority of the Word, but rather to recognize that the report given is an accurate one about what Job and his friends believed.)

2. From the Book of Job, reconstruct the concepts of morality accepted by believers of that day. How does this statement correspond with New Testament moral concepts? What issues are "moral" issues to them? What standards govern the content of morality?

3. Write a letter, building on what you have learned from Job, to a person who is tormented by the feeling that a recent tragedy must be God punishing him for sin.

THE PROMISE

ABRAHAM STANDS AS THE GREATEST FIGURE to be found in the ancient world. Three world religions—Islam, Judaism and Christianity—revere him as the father of their faith. Archaeologists have explored the city of his origin, traced his journeys, probed the ruins of towns mentioned in Genesis and reconstructed a striking portrait of life 2,000 years before Christ that in detail after detail confirms the accuracy of the Old Testament account.

But what makes Abraham important to the Bible student is not the reverence in which he's held today. Nor is it, as *The National Geographic* once suggested, that "Abraham the Patriarch conceived a great and simple idea: the idea of a single, almighty God."[1] His importance is not even found in the fact that Abraham stands today as a model

1. Kenneth MacLeish, "Abraham, the Friend of God," *National Geographic,* Dec. 1966, p. 740.

of faith, a sharp and clear illustration of the truth that God gives salvation to ungodly men on the basis of their trust in Him.

No, the importance of Abraham here in Genesis is that through Abraham God reveals a deeper purpose and goal for the universe. To Abraham God revealed that He has a plan. To Abraham promises were given which show us history's direction. In Abraham we first discover that the personal universe described in the early chapters of Genesis is a purposive universe as well!

The promise. Genesis 11: 10-32 traces the genealogy of the man who is to become such a key to understanding the Old Testament. We read of his birthplace. Acts 7: 2 tells of a journey that he began when God first spoke to him and instructed him to leave Mesopotamia to go to a land God would show him. Abraham left. While pausing in Haran along the way, God spoke again, repeating His command (12: 1), and adding words of promise. In a series of great "I will's," God stated an unshakable purpose which has remained constant through the millenniums, and which is the foundation on which our grasp of Old and New Testament revelations must rest today. All the Old Testament and the New can be understood as a progressive unfolding of the purpose God first announced to Abraham some 4,000 years ago.

Yet, glancing at the words in Genesis 12, we're apt to miss this significance. It is only as we note the restatement of the promises that come periodically throughout the Old Testament that we begin to see their implications. As we hear the words of promise developed by the prophets, we see how completely central this revelation of purpose is. As we take this promise as a literal and changeless expression of God's purpose, the relationship between the Old and New Testaments becomes clear. And the history of our own day, as we await the return of Christ, is suddenly filled with fresh meaning.

The Genesis promises stand.

They are at the root of the Jewish identity through the millenniums. They are the key to understanding the Old Testament. They are a window on current events.

"I will." These words introduce the promise as expressed in Genesis 12: 2, 3. The details are unclear at this point. But the general shape of the purpose is taking form.

I will make you a great nation. From Abraham, Arab and Jew trace their origins. More than one nation now calls Abraham "father."

I will bless you and make your name great. The reverence of millions in the three great monotheistic faiths has more than fulfilled this word.

I will make you a blessing. From Abraham came the people of Israel. From Israel came both our Scriptures and our Savior.

I will bless those who bless you, and curse those who curse you. In striking ways, the rise and fall of empires bear out the stated intention of God to deal with men and nations as they deal with His chosen.

In you will all the families of the earth be blessed. God's choice of Abraham and his children was not designed to exclude others. From the very beginning God's choice of Israel was announced for the benefit of mankind. And on the return of Christ, the King, the fullness of blessing will be extended to all.

There is a final promise, one added after Abraham had responded in faith and left Haran, finally entering the land of Canaan. The Lord appeared and said:

To your descendants I will give THIS land. The purposes of God and the future of Israel are focused on a particular place: a land, Palestine, where in our own day we've seen the planting once again of a Jewish state.

TRACING THE PROMISE

The statement of promise found in Genesis 12 is only a first faint outline of the divine purpose which gives shape to the Old Testament and to the history of the world. As we read on in the Bible we realize that these first promises give the Jewish people their sense of identity. Then these first promises are developed. At critical times in the history of Israel, various dimensions of God's purpose are amplified and revealed.

So it's helpful to look ahead and to see briefly some dimensions of the promise and purpose first presented in Genesis.

Genesis 15. The promises given Abraham must

have placed a strain on his faith, for Abraham and Sarah were childless. As was common in that culture, Abraham had designated Eliezer of Damascus (who probably had the status of an adopted son), to be his heir and care for his wife should he die. In Genesis 15 the question is raised by Abraham: How could the announced purpose of God be fulfilled since he was childless?

In 15: 4 is God's response: "Your own son shall be your heir." God's promises would be passed on to Abraham's physical seed, and that seed would be as impossible for man to number as the stars of the heaven are to count (15: 5).

Here, too, God defines the extent of the land to be given Abraham's descendants: "from the river of Egypt to the great river, the river Euphrates" (15: 18). The land was further defined for Abraham by listing the peoples who then lived within it (see map following page).

Genesis 17. Years had passed since Abraham had been given the initial promises, years during which he and his wife Sarah had no children. Finally, some 12 years before the scene sketched in this chapter, Abraham, following established custom of his time, had fathered a son by Hagar, his wife's servant. The child, Ishmael (progenitor of the Arabs), was rejected as the heir to the promise. Instead God changes Abram's name (meaning "father") to Abraham (meaning "father of a multitude"). This 99-year-old man was told that he and Sarah, who was then 90 and beyond childbearing years, would have a son of their own. This

117

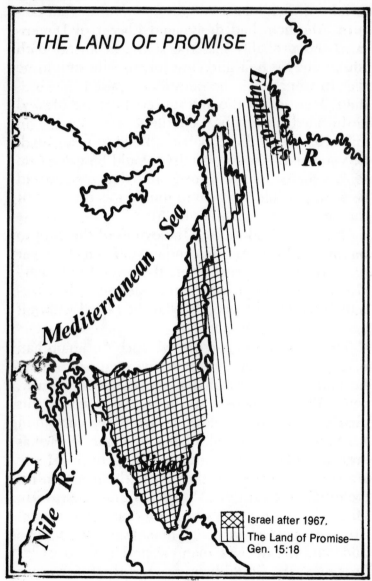

THE LAND OF PROMISE

Israel after 1967.
The Land of Promise—
Gen. 15:18

child of miracle was to be named Isaac, and he was to inherit the promises.

In this statement of promise, two new dimensions are added. First, the special relationship with Abraham's descendants is to be an everlasting one, "throughout their generations" (17: 7). Second, the title deed to Palestine is given the same "everlasting" status. As history has demonstrated, sin might cause Israel to be expelled from the land. But the title to it is retained. The promises made to Abraham, and the purposes they express, are to be viewed as changeless.

II Samuel 7. Centuries passed before another significant amplification of the original promise was made. In the early days of Israel's organization as a monarchy, David was selected to be king and special promises were given to him. His line was to be established as the royal line, and from his descendants was to come an Offspring whose Kingdom would be established forever (7: 12, 13). A Davidic ruler might not always sit on a throne in Jerusalem, but there would always be a rightful heir until finally the promised King would ascend the throne to rule over an endless Kingdom.

From the perspective given by the New Testament, the promise becomes strikingly clear. Matthew carefully traces the line of David to Jesus. Even today the rightful Heir lives. And one day soon, He, Jesus of Nazareth, will take the throne. The eternal purposes of God in Israel will be fulfilled and the promises kept through Jesus' reign.

Jeremiah 30, 31. Still more centuries followed.

119

The people of God were torn from the Promised Land and dragged into captivity. Then Jeremiah was used by God to add yet another dimension to the purpose.

In the chapters of the Book of Jeremiah, the Abrahamic promise is reconfirmed. God will bring the captive people back to the Promised Land (30: 3). What's more, the promise to David is reconfirmed as well. A Davidic King will be raised up as Israel's Ruler and relate God to man (30: 9, 21). And now comes the new revelation.

Long after Abraham, God had given his descendants a Law to keep. The Law was given to provide evidence of faith's obedience and was the basis on which a particular generation of Jews might expect blessing or judgment. Obedience meant that that generation would have a present experience of the blessings promised for history's end. Disobedience meant that though the promise was sure, that generation would suffer judgment.

Through Jeremiah now comes a revelation of the fact that the fulfillment of promise deals not only with the external life of men but with the inner man as well. The promise is not simply for the day of peace and plenty which men yearn for. The promise of God involves conversion: the gift of a new heart and a new personal relationship with God that will mend the ravages of sin upon the human personality (Jer. 31: 31-35). The promise to Abraham is ultimately related to the undoing of the curse. The very sin that mars the image of God in man will be dealt with, iniquity forgiven and washed away and a new heart restored in full harmony with God and godliness.

Through Abraham's race God intends to purify mankind!

It is here that the line of promise spills over into the New Testament revelation. In the Second Coming of Christ we see the appearance of the promised King. In the Cross we see the reconciliation of mankind. Thus in this one Person God is working out His purpose and His plan. In this one Person God intends "to bring all things in heaven and on earth together under one head, even Christ" (Eph. 1: 10, NIV). This total purpose of God, which the later millennia have revealed, lies latent in the seed of promise planted in Genesis 12.

A COVENANT

Our understanding of the significance of these promises is heightened when we realize that they were given specific expression as *covenants*.

The covenant was the contract of the ancient world. Agreements between parties were given binding status by the "cutting" or making of a covenant. While there were several forms for making a covenant, the most binding of all was the "covenant of blood." Animals were killed and divided (hence the term "cutting" a covenant), and both parties to the treaty passed between the pieces, thus binding themselves to its provisions. It is such a solemnizing of God's promise to Abraham we read of in Genesis 15. Keil and Delitzsch note, "Thus God condescended to follow the custom of the Chaldeans, that He might in the most solemn manner confirm His oath to Abram the Chaldean."[2]

What is so significant about the Genesis 15 scene is not so much its conformity with ancient practice as its one-party nature. In the normal covenant relationship two parties entered into a conditional relationship. If one failed to perform as required, the other was freed from his responsibility as well. But the Bible tells us that God caused a deep sleep to come upon Abraham, and only the Lord passed between the sacrifices. God had announced a purpose that no act of man could alter. Now God confirmed the promise that His purpose would be fulfilled through Abraham's seed. There were no conditions laid on Abraham or them. God and God only pressed His seal on the contract made and witnessed that day. Looking back, the New Testament comments:

> When God made his promise to Abraham, since there was no one greater for him to swear by, he swore by himself, saying, "I will surely bless you and give you many descendants." Men swear by someone greater than themselves, and the oath confirms what is said and puts an end to all argument. Because God wanted to make the unchanging nature of his

2. C. F. Keil and Franz Delitzsch, *The Pentateuch* (Edinburgh: T. & T. Clark, 1886), 1: 214.

purpose very clear to the heirs of what was promised, he confirmed it with an oath. God did this so that, by two unchangeable things in which it is impossible for God to lie, we who have fled to take hold of the hope offered to us may be greatly encouraged.

Hebrews 6: 13, 14, 16-18 (NIV)

The promise *is* clear. Confirmed with an oath, the purpose of God as it begins to take shape in the promise to Abraham is unchangeable and sure.

Unchangeable. Across the years Bible students have argued concerning the various elements of God's purpose introduced in the Genesis chapters. Some have felt that the promises are fulfilled in the Christian Church, the "spiritual seed" of Abraham whose faith in God we share.

But it's difficult to explain away that which God takes such care to define.

Who are the descendants of Abraham as far as the Covenant promise is concerned? Not Eliezer, no matter how deeply he may have shared the faith of Abraham. Not Ishmael, although Abraham was his physical father. But Isaac, a child of Abraham in both senses—physical and spiritual!

What is the land? Not mountaintop experiences or milk and honey spiritual provision, but the actual land of Palestine, marked out by geographical boundaries and defined by the names of tribes and cities still reflected in the place names of our own day.

On what basis might God break the promises?

None, for an unconditional contract had been made. God bound Himself and Himself alone "to make the unchanging nature of his purpose very clear" (Heb. 6: 17, NIV).

After that contract was ratified, Scripture continues to give witness to its unbreakable character. In Genesis 17: 7 God says the promise is "everlasting." After a long age of apostasy, the Covenant is confirmed and David is given the promise of the throne "forever." At the very moment of Israel's expulsion from the land for apostasy and idolatry, the Covenants are confirmed and even greater promises added through Jeremiah, with the unconditional character of the Covenant emphasized (31: 35-38).

No, the purpose once expressed has not been changed. God does have a direction for history, a direction tied up in the experience of a chosen race, a race chosen to be a channel through which God would bless the world.

THE DOMINANT THEME

Why have we spent so much time looking at the promise here in Genesis? Because the concept of this Covenant, the idea that God chose Israel and made certain promises to it that reveal His eternal purposes, dominates the Old Testament. And because God's purposes as expressed in the promise are unchangeable, it is to the Old Testament we must look for a key to understand our own day and current events.

The concept of this Covenant also helps us in the study of the rest of Genesis. The stories of two of the patriarchs, Isaac and Jacob, are not told simply because these men were "interesting," or even because they were believers through whose lives we can learn. No, Isaac and Jacob are significant in Genesis because these men are inheritors of the divine promise. In them we see the preservation of the promise, and to them Israel traced the title deed to Palestine and their identity as the people of God. Later, as a mob of millions struggled out of Egyptian slavery, Moses would remind them of their origin and of their destiny: a nation called to reveal God to a world that lived without understanding and without hope.

GOING DEEPER

to personalize

In the next chapters we'll look at Abraham's life and times and at his personal relationship with God. But in this study we need to focus on the Abrahamic Covenant, that oath-confirmed promise God gave Abraham and his descendants.

1. Psalms 111 and 136 portray how God's Old Testament people saw and worshiped Him. Read them carefully and see if you can find evidence of the anchor that these believers found for their faith in the Lord's revelation of Himself as a covenant-keeping God.

2. Study the following passages carefully, listing

for each the elements of promise emphasized. Genesis 12: 1-3; 15: 1-21; 17: 1-8.

3. Study Hebrews 6: 13-20. How does the revelation of God as a covenant-keeping God relate to you and your faith in Him today?

to probe

1. Some people today believe that the Covenant made with Abraham was conditional as far as his earthly or physical seed was concerned. When the people of Israel sinned and turned from God, it is suggested that God turned from them to keep the promises in a spiritual seed, the Christian Church. From a study of the Covenant promises in the Old Testament, would you tend to agree or disagree with this theory? Why?

2. Look at the passage dealing with circumcision as a sign of keeping the Covenant (Gen. 17). Is this "condition" something added as man's part to the basic promise? How can it be understood?

This prayer, offered by faithful Jews who even today circumcise on the eighth day, shows how the Hebrews view circumcision and gives an answer to the "condition" concept questioned above:

Blessed are You, Lord our God, Master of the Universe, who have made us holy with Your Commandments, and have commanded us to bring this boy into the covenant of Abraham our Father.

ABRAHAM:
ALL TOO HUMAN

SKIMMING THE ANCIENT NARRATIVE portraying Abraham's life and times, it's difficult to gain a clear perspective. In some ways the familiar events seem to have happened only yesterday. In others, the stories are timeless; they seem divorced from reality.

But the man Abraham did live in our world, in our history. When Abraham was born in the 2160s B.C.[1] there were tribal groups roaming Europe gathering nuts and berries, without written language or national boundary. It would be another 1,400 years before the traditional date for the founding of Rome, the so-called "Eternal City"! When the baby Abraham cried out for milk, China's first known dynasty, the Hsia was just

1. Scholars differ on dates for Abraham. Some would date him as late as the 18th century B.C. However, for our purposes, we have accepted the system of dating found in Leon Wood's *A Survey of Israel's History* (Grand Rapids: Zondervan, 1970).

formed. It would be nearly 1,000 years before any now surviving Chinese literature would be penned.

Yet Abraham's world was the seat of an advanced civilization. In the 400 years before Abraham, Egypt's culture had flourished. When Abraham walked our world, the pyramids were nearly new—giant blocks of rock unscoured by desert sands. Yet, by Abraham's time, Egypt was suffering economic and political depression, conditions stimulating a significant literature. Canaan had been a flourishing land of urbanized city-states a mere hundred years or so before Abraham. But by the time he was a man, the barbarian Amorites had wasted much of the land, and the population, except in some of the valleys, had become scarce and nomadic.

Archaeology has provided an impressive picture of Ur, Abraham's early home. This city of about half a million people was a center of culture. It boasted an extensive library, an elaborate postal system, a busy port and factories. Its people lived under a code of just laws, knew economic stability (though they did suffer from some inflation) and their children went to schools where reading and other subjects were taught. Settled in comfortable two-story homes they had a form of air conditioning. The people enjoyed a complex civilization, attested by the over 100,000 business documents that, in addition to religious texts and hymns, still survive.

Jewish tradition portrays Abraham as a cultured

and sophisticated man. All we know of his origin reinforces this picture. When Europe lay in darkness, when Chinese civilization was being born, God reached out to touch a man who lived in the world's center of culture. A real man. A man of history. Abraham.

VISIT TO A STRANGE COUNTRY

Even today when we visit a foreign country we confront customs and folkways easily misunderstood. Imagine then a visit to the world of Abraham, some 4,000 years and uncounted generations away. No wonder some of the things we read of in Genesis seem strange!

But the science of archaeology, which for decades concentrated its efforts in the Middle Eastern world, has provided many insights. Through discoveries of codes of law and custom, business contracts, letters, etc., we can understand many otherwise inexplicable events of Abraham's life. Thus it's helpful to note the actions explained by our discoveries about the ancient world, discoveries that will help you as you continue reading now in the Biblical text.

Genesis 11: 31–12: 9. Abraham's journey was along well-established trade routes connecting Ur with Haran, Palestine, the Mediterranean coast and Egypt. Even the towns Abraham visited lie in rainfall zones with annual inches of rain sufficient to support the sheep and herds he brought along.

Genesis 12: 10-20. Abraham's fear that Pharaoh

FIGURE IV

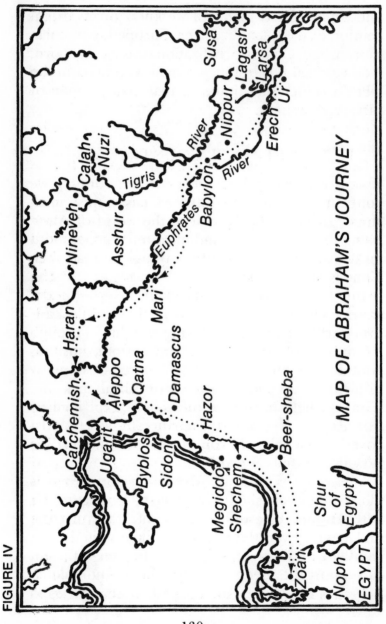

MAP OF ABRAHAM'S JOURNEY

might kill him to obtain Sarah has some precedent. There is record of a pharaoh doing just this in the case of a visitor from the north.

Genesis 13. Lot went against custom when he failed to give Abraham, his elder, first choice, even though it had been offered to him. Lot chose the more prosperous and populated valley areas; Abraham received less populated hill country.

Genesis 14. Until recent years the story of the invasion of the five kings reported here was questioned by liberal scholars. Archaeology has now shown that kings from as far away as lower Mesopotamia (see Abraham's Journey map) did make such incursions, and both people and place names fit those of Abraham's time. Even the reason for such invasions is now known: copper, manganese and asphalt were valuable natural resources of the region.

Genesis 15. The Nuzi tablets, about 20,000, documents written on hardened clay discovered in 1925-31, date within 400 or 500 years of the patriarchs. They show customs like those mentioned in Scripture. One custom involves adoption of a slave or freeman who in return for serving his benefactor becomes his heir. The contract of adoption also contained provisions stating that if the patron later had a son, the son would be the heir. This is reflected in 15: 1-4, with Eliezer the designated "heir of my [Abraham's] house".

Genesis 16. Ten years after the promise of a son to be Abraham's heir, Sarah follows custom in suggesting that Abraham take her maid, Hagar, as a secondary wife. This was by custom a moral action, and may have seemed to Abraham as the way God would keep His promise. But it was not God's plan.

Sarah's later bitterness and her insistence that Hagar and Ishmael be expelled went directly *against* custom (21: 10). God had to personally intervene to move Abraham to do what he felt was wrong.

Abraham's statement in 16: 6, "Your maid is in your power," was not permission to mistreat Hagar but recognition of the existing legal right of Sarah to "deal harshly" with a slave.

Genesis 18. The picture of Abraham and Sarah themselves preparing a meal for the three strangers reflects a cultural stress on hospitality.

Genesis 19. The city gate, where Lot met the two angels who came to search out the righteous in Sodom, was a place where men of the ancient world gathered to talk, conduct business and settle disputes. It was the focus of the city life.

The heavy doors on Lot's own house (vs. 9) are also interesting. Archaeologists have found that homes of a later date were not hung with heavy doors. But homes in Palestine in Abraham's day were so protected.

Leon Wood describes the destruction of Sodom and Gomorrah and shows how the Biblical description fits geological and other data:

The destruction of Sodom was effected by a rain of "brimstone and fire." In examining the meaning of this expression, scholars have ruled out volcanic action on the basis of negative geological indications. Many believe that it refers to an earthquake resulting in an enormous explosion. Several factors are pointed out as favoring the view. The idea of brimstone and fire suggests incendiary materials raining down upon the city as the result of an explosion. Another descriptive word used is "overthrew" (Gen. 19: 29), and this fits the thought of an earthquake. That Abraham saw smoke rising in the direction of the city indicates that there was fire. Inflammable asphalt has long been known in the area. Records from ancient writers speak of strong sulpheric odors, which suggest that quantities of sulphur were there in past time. Further, the whole Jordan Valley constitutes an enormous fault in the earth's surface, given to earthquake conditions. It is possible, then, that God did see fit to miraculously time an earthquake at this precise moment, which could have released great quantities of gas, mixed sulphur with various salts found in abundance, and measurably increased the flow of asphalt seepage. Had lightning ignited it all, the entire country would have been consumed as indicated.[2]

The action of Lot's daughters after the destruc-

2. Ibid., p. 56.

tion finds no justification in custom or ancient culture.

Genesis 21. Even though Sarah was upset by the 15-year-old Ishmael teasing her two-year-old (vs. 9, TLB), there was no excuse in custom for her insistence that Ishmael and his mother be sent away with no part of Abraham's wealth. In fact, custom insisted that Ishmael be provided for. No wonder it "was very displeasing to Abraham" (vs. 11). God intervened to promise Abraham that He would care for Ishmael and make him a nation too. Only then was Abraham willing to expel the two.

ALL TOO HUMAN

The survey of customs of Abraham's day may help us understand some of the events recorded in Scripture. But custom does not explain away flaws we discover in Abraham's character! And it's important, before we see Abraham as a man of faith, to realize that he was, like you and me, far from perfect.

Sometimes we forget this and tend to idealize the people of the Bible. We even try to explain away the faults we're shown in the Word. Sometimes we hold up men—rather than God—as examples of perfection.

It's difficult to do this with Abraham. In too many ways Abraham is revealed to be a man with human faults. And we need to be just as blunt as Scripture is in recognizing and examining them.

We have an early indication of his flaws in Genesis 12. Abram had been called by God to go to a land which the Lord Himself chose. He had obeyed in an act that required real faith. But once in the land, Abram's faith was shaken by a famine. Rather than trust God or wait for further direction, he went to Egypt. There he continued to show lack of trust by getting Sarah to tell a half-truth about their relationship, to deny that she was his wife. Fear that he might be killed outweighed his commitment to his wife. Even when she was taken into Pharoah's household. Abram did not reveal their relationship. Instead he profited in silence from the favor extended to the supposed brother!

Abraham's tendency to rely on his wits rather than on God is also shown in the events leading up to the birth of Ishmael. Some ten years had passed as Abraham waited for the son God promised. Finally Sarah began urging him to take her maid as a secondary wife. Even though this was a custom of the land, it took Sarah's nagging to make him take action. He "hearkened to [obeyed!] the voice of Sarai" (16: 2). Perhaps Abraham thought that he would "help" God keep His promises. Perhaps he felt that 86 was just too old to wait any longer. In any case, Abraham did not consult God. He simply went ahead, without direction, relying on his own plans to fulfill God's purposes. Self-reliance and self-effort took the place of trust in God.

And then, how stunning. Abraham repeats the

sin he did in Egypt! Again Abraham misrepresents Sarah as only his sister, and she is placed in the harem of a king named Abimelech. God protects Sarah even though her husband is unwilling to, and before Abimelech approached her God spoke to him in a vision. Abimelech, fearful at the divine visitation, complains to Abraham that he might have led him into unknowing sin. Abraham's response is weak (Gen. 20: 11, 12). Abraham feared for his life, not for his wife. He worried that the people of the strange place might not fear God and thus might kill him for Sarah. Abraham apparently did not even stop to think that although a particular people might not know God, God knew them! There was no place Abraham could go to be beyond the protection of the Lord. Yet, even after an earlier rebuke in Egypt, Abraham repeated the same sin and let fear and selfishness control his choices.

No, the Abraham we meet on the pages of the Bible is not an idealized man. He is a man we need to see as both a weak and a willful sinner.

Not good? The normal reaction at this point is to object. We want to point out some of the many good traits Abraham exhibits to balance the portrait of the sinner. We want to stress Abraham's initial trust in God. His generosity with Lot. His refusal to risk God's glory when offered the loot of Sodom.

And we can find things to praise Abraham for. In this too Abraham is like each of us. Not totally bad—not totally good. A strange mixture of admirable traits, and traits that must in honesty be labeled as despicable. Abraham is a man whose best traits are flawed by the mark of Adam's sin. In him as well as in us weakness and willfulness combine. God's image is there, but so is the unmistakable stamp of sin.

It is just this fact that makes Abraham such an important illustration of Bible truth. No, he cannot be held up as an illustration of the goodness of man. He is, instead, an example of the fact that God cares for, and gives His salvation to, the unworthy!

In later centuries Abraham's descendants would miss this message. The men of Israel would look back and claim God's favor as their birthright on the basis of their descent from Abraham and on the basis of their possession of the Law. They would not, as Abraham did, admit sin and need and come to God with no pretensions of ability to earn His favor. They would not be willing, as Abraham was, to bow as a sinner before God and to trust God alone in order that faith might be counted for righteousness.

This is Paul's point in Romans 4:1-5 (NIV):

What then shall we say that Abraham, our forefather, discovered in this matter? If, in fact, Abraham was justified by works, he had something to boast about—but not before God. What does the Scripture say: "Abraham believed God, and it was credited to him as righteousness." Now when a man works, his wages are not credited to him as a gift, but as an obligation. However, to the man who does not work but trusts God who justifies the wicked, his faith is credited as righteousness.

God, who justifies the wicked. It is in this way that you and I first need to see Abraham. We need to look at him as the Bible shows him to be in order to explain so many of his failures and sins. And it is in his failures that you and I can find comfort!

For our failures and our sins are just as real as his were. Like Abraham, we need to turn away from our own works to rely on God alone. "This," says Romans, "is why 'it was credited to him [Abraham] as righteousness.' The words 'it was credited to him' were written not for him alone, but also for us, to whom God will credit righteousness—for us who believe in him who raised Jesus our Lord from the dead" (4: 22-24, NIV).

And so in Abraham we have a mirror—of ourselves. And we have a message from God. As Abraham did, we need to turn from any hope in our own goodness and find in God's message about Jesus our own way to faith's escape.

GOING DEEPER

to personalize

   1. Reread Genesis 12—21, giving each chapter a

title to reflect the way that it portrays Abraham.

2. Look through Genesis 12—21 for Abraham's good traits. What in him is admirable?

3. Try now to identify yourself with Abraham. In what ways are you like him both in his failures and his good qualities?

to probe

1. Locate several books on Bible customs and on archaeology of the Old Testament. Check them to see what help they give in understanding these Genesis chapters.

2. Select one of the following passages and write a brief commentary. In it discuss insights from archaeology, the portrait of Abraham given here, questions likely to be raised by readers and application of the passage to believers today.

   a. Genesis 13

   b. Genesis 18: 16-33

   c. Genesis 20

10

BY FAITH

IT'S FUN FOR MY WIFE and me to sit down and remember our oldest son as a child (he's in college now). We can laugh as we remember the adventures he had, like the time he and a friend penetrated the defenses of the natural gas company near our Illinois home and were given a guided tour of the fenced-in area. Or the time Paul won the math blue ribbon in a competition with other schools. Or the hours upon hours he and I spent in the front yard wearing away our grass as we played football. Looking back, there are things that stand out, highlights that focus on his positive traits.

In the New Testament, God looks back on the days of Genesis to reminisce about His child, Abraham. Like my wife and I, God focuses on the positive traits. Somehow the weaknesses and failures that also were part of Abraham's personality are overlooked. Forgiveness and that blood spilled on Calvary have freed God to forget.

But what does God remember? What does the New Testament emphasize as the central message in Abraham's life? What is emphasized is not that he, like us, was a lost sinner, but that Abraham was lifted beyond himself by faith!

Hebrews 11: 8-19 (NIV) focuses on three events in Abraham's life that God fondly remembers:

By faith, Abraham, when called to go to a place he would later receive as his possession, obeyed and went, even though he did not know where he was going. By faith he made his home in the promised land like a stranger in a foreign country; he lived in tents, as did Isaac and Jacob, who were heirs with him of the same promise. For he was looking forward to the city with foundations, whose architect and builder is God.

By faith Abraham, even though he was past age—and Sarah herself was barren—was enabled to become a father because he considered him faithful who had made the promise. And so from this one man, and he as good as dead, came descendants as numerous as the stars in the sky and as countless as the sand of the seashore. . . .

By faith Abraham, when God tested him, offered Isaac as a sacrifice. He who had received the promises was about to sacrifice his one and only son, even though God had said to him, "Through Isaac shall your promised offspring come." Abraham reasoned that God could raise the dead, and figuratively speaking, he did receive Isaac back from death.

These three times when reason might well have challenged the spoken word of God, Abraham responded with faith.

It is here, in Abraham's faith-response to God, that we find this basic Bible theme brought into clear focus. Earlier God had affirmed His existence and His care for men. He had spoken to individuals before, like Noah and Cain. But it is in Abraham that we discover a clear illustration of what has always separated mankind's Noahs from its Cains. It isn't that Noah was a "better" man or that Cain was intrinsically "worse." Both were men of mixed character. Both did good things, yet found reflected in their actions the taint of sin.

No, what sets men apart as far as relationship with God is concerned always has been a simple thing: faith. Noah trusted God and built an ark in which he and his family were saved. Cain refused to trust God. This led directly to his final bondage to sin, a servitude whose full expression is found in the murder of his brother.

Faith divides man from man. The way you and I respond to God as He speaks His message to us is the critical issue of our life. This message we hear in the story of Abraham. From Abraham we learn much of the nature of that faith which pleases God and frees Him to act in our lives today.

ABRAHAM'S FAITH

The three incidents recalled in Hebrews 11 now become the focus of our study of Abraham as well as the key to understanding how his experiences minister God's message to us today.

Abraham obeyed and went (Gen. 12). It would be wrong to picture Abraham as an adventurous man eager to travel. It would also be a mistake to see him as a crusader, a man gripped with the vision of one God which he was determined to transplant to another land. The Bible says that when the family lived "beyond the Euphrates, Terah, the father of Abraham and of Nahor; and they served other gods" (Josh. 24: 2). During the first 75 years of his life, Abraham lived in a pagan world and prospered. There's no reason to suppose that when God spoke to him Abraham was other than a successful businessman who enjoyed considerable wealth and a comfortable life in the center of the world's civilization.

Even today, when people move so often, it's difficult for a person to be uprooted. God's call to Abraham demanded total restructuring of his life-style. He left his own civilization for a foreign land. He left a place of culture to move to the backward home of wanderers. He left his air-conditioned home to take up residence in a tent. He left stability for the uncertainty of travel and ever-changing circumstances. He left the security of an established code of laws to wander, afraid, from land to land (cf. Gen. 20: 11). He left a long tradition of worship of Nanna, the moon god, for a God who had spoken to him, but whom he did not yet know.

Leaving Ur was an act of faith. In making this difficult decision Abraham exhibited a unique trust.

In some ways each of us makes this kind of decision when we first trust Christ as Savior. Our lives have developed a pattern, sometimes one that is well established. We don't really know what the Christian experience may bring, or where God is leading. So we take a risk. We give up the familiar for the strange. We, too, leave our past for a "land we know not of." The beginning of Abraham's pilgrimage is a picture of the beginning of each man's pilgrimage into Christ.

Abraham considered Him faithful (Gen. 15). We see the next great act of faith in Genesis 15. God has given Abraham great promises which hinge on the founding of a family line. But Abraham is childless. When Abraham raises this question with God, the Lord promises, "Your own son shall be your heir" (15: 4). God then goes on to promise Abraham uncountable descendants. The text tells us, "He believed the Lord; and he reckoned it to him as righteousness" (vs. 6).

The New Testament emphasizes the great trust this act of faith required. "Without weakening in his faith, he faced the fact that his body was as good as dead—since he was about a hundred years old—and that Sarah's womb was also dead. Yet he did not waver through unbelief regarding the promise of God, but was strengthened in his faith and gave glory to God, being fully persuaded that God had power to do what he had promised" (Rom. 4: 19-21, NIV).

In this event we gain deep insight into saving faith. Faith faces the facts. Abraham had no illusions about his own ability to father a son, or Sarah's to become a mother. Physically speaking this was impossible. The two were, as far as the ability to become parents, "as good as dead." Yet Abraham's kind of faith also faces the fact of God. And God changes every equation! Abraham stands here as evidence that God *can* be trusted to keep His Word, and that such trust is never disappointed.

Several factors need to be noted to grasp the message God is communicating:

■ *The promises.* Abraham is not exercising blind faith. Instead, he is responding to a word spoken by the Lord. It is the concrete, objective expression of God's promise that calls for response.

"Faith" in what we imagine to be God's will is not Abraham's kind of faith. Abraham's faith is a response to divine revelation.

■ *The Person.* Abraham's confidence is in God as a Person who is both able and committed to do what He has promised. Sometimes we think of "faith" as subjective, something *we* do. Abraham's kind of faith does not rely on its own intensity or sincerity. Abraham's kind of faith puts reliance on the object of faith: God Himself. It is God's trustworthiness and not our trusting that is critical.

■ *The perspective.* Abraham boldly faced the fact of

his and Sarah's age. He realistically looked at the situation, and just as realistically ignored the circumstances! Realism understands that physical and other limitations do not apply to God, for God is the underlying reality; and whatever the circumstances, God can bring to pass what He promises.

Abraham might very well have cried out, "I can't!" And he would have been right. Instead Abraham affirmed, "God can!" This perspective, which sees God as the touchstone of reality, is to characterize our faith as well.

■ *The product.* God announced it: "It was credited to him as righteousness" (Rom. 4: 22, NIV). Like you and I, Abraham was not a righteous man. There was no basis on which God and Abraham could have fellowship until God revealed that He would accept faith and, because of it, credit Abraham's account with righteousness.

More is involved here than a divine bookkeeping transaction. Through faith God works to produce righteousness in us. As we learn to live by Abraham's kind of faith, facing each test and trial with our eyes on God and His trustworthiness, God the Holy Spirit produces in our lives the fruit of a righteousness which we ourselves do not possess (Gal. 5: 18-23). God counts faith as holiness and through faith produces the very holiness He has promised is—and will be—ours.

Abraham reasoned (Gen. 22). This is one of the most unusual and, at the same time, most exciting stories in the Bible. Isaac, the promised heir, has

147

been born, and he now plays by Abraham's tent entrance. The old man has grown to dearly love this child for whom he waited so long with such eager expectation. Suddenly, as if to shatter the old man's world, God speaks to him again: "Take your son, your only son Isaac, whom you love, and go to the land of Moriah, and offer him there as a burnt offering upon one of the mountains of which I shall tell you" (Genesis 22: 2).

Then the Bible tells us an amazing thing: "Abraham rose early in the morning, saddled his ass, and took two of his young men with him, and his son Isaac; and he cut the wood for the burnt offering, and arose and went to the place of which God had told him" (22: 3).

There was no hesitation. Abraham obeyed.

We can't know how Abraham felt on the three-day journey, or the doubts and fears that may have stormed his heart and mind. But we do know that before he arrived, Abraham had worked the problem through. The New Testament tells us "Abraham reasoned that God could raise the dead" (Heb. 11: 19, NIV). Abraham knew that God had promised, "Through Isaac shall your promised offspring come" (vs. 18, NIV). God would not go back on His stated word. If God chose to accept Isaac as a sacrifice, Abraham would give him, sure that somehow God would give the child back to him again.

And so the Genesis text reveals in a Hebrew plural word which is lost in our English translation: "Stay here," Abraham tells the servants who accompanied him. "I and the lad will go yonder and worship, and [we will] come again to you" (22:5). Abraham did not know the means, but he did know that God would provide.

God did. As Abraham was about to plunge the knife into the bound body of his son, the Lord stopped him and pointed out a ram whose horns had been caught in a thicket. The ram was slain, the boy loosed. God Himself had provided a substitute.

And then God spoke again. The testing was complete. God's promises to Abraham were reconfirmed and Abraham, his trust also confirmed by the events, returned with Isaac to their tents.

What is there in this story for us? Much.

■ *Faith's life.* The life of faith that God calls us to is not an easy one. Like Abraham we may well be called on to make heartrending decisions. But also like Abraham, we can fix our confidence securely in God.

■ *A reasoned faith.* Faith is not opposed to reason. The man who relies on God simply takes more into account in his reasoning than the man who does not believe. Often an appeal to "reason" means no more than insistence on considering only what a person can see and touch and feel.

We all face this danger. In the decisions you and I face, do we look only at factors we can see? Or do we reason that God is able to alter circumstances to fit His will? Abraham reasoned that God's will is the ultimate reality and that God's expressed purposes are sure. It was this kind of reasoning—that takes God into account—that was

149

part of Abraham's faith. And it must become a part of ours.

■ *An unhesitant faith.* Abraham did not wait. He "rose up early" to act in obedience to God's will. An overt response to God's Word is still an integral part of what "faith" is to mean. Often our feelings and desires struggle against our intention to respond to God. But trust in God as a Person not only frees us to respond; our actions give evidence of the reality of our trust.

Abraham's journey to Mount Moriah is portrayed in Scripture as a test. It was a test that Abraham passed, and in passing, demonstrated to God, to himself, to Isaac—and to us—the reality of his faith in God.

FAITH TODAY

Faith is a major theme of both Testaments. And all that the New Testament explains finds full expression in Abraham's faith.

Today faith opens up the way to a personal relationship with God. Paul argues in Romans, "We maintain that a man is justified by faith apart from observing the law" (3: 28, NIV). Abraham was a man who sinned. In Romans 1-3, Paul proves that all share this nature with him. Abraham received great promises from God. We, too, have received a promise in Jesus, God's Son. "God presented him as a sacrifice of atonement, through faith in his blood" (Rom. 3: 25, NIV). God promises us that, on the basis of Jesus' death for us, He will forgive and transform the person who relies on Christ alone for salvation. Abraham trusted God, and this trust was accepted by the Lord and credited to him as a righteousness he did not have. These words, " 'It was credited to him' were written . . . also for us, to whom God will credit righteousness—for us who believe in him who raised Jesus our Lord from the dead" (4: 23, 24, NIV).

Today, too, faith is evidenced in our actions. In a passage that troubles many, the Bible insists, "Faith that doesn't show itself by good works is no faith at all—it is dead and useless" (Jas. 2: 17, TLB). The writer asks,"Was not our ancestor Abraham considered righteous for what he did when he offered his son Isaac on the altar? You see," James continues, "that his faith was made complete by what he did. And the scripture was fulfilled that says, 'Abraham believed God, and it was credited to him as righteousness,' and he was called God's friend. You see that a person is justified by what he does and not by faith alone" (2: 21-24, NIV).

It's important to note the author's concern in this passage. James is combating a notion common in our day as well: that "faith" means "agree to" or "believe about." It's easy to say we believe that Jesus actually lived and died and was raised again. It's something else to say that we have trusted ourselves to Him, as Abraham trusted himself to God. Yet it is in the sense of *trusting ourselves to* that the

Bible uses "faith" when speaking of a relationship with God.

The question then comes: What is the difference between "belief about" and a "trusting in"? The answer is sharp and clear: The one who trusts will demonstrate his faith by his actions. This was certainly true in the case of Abraham. How was Abraham able to get up early in the morning and set out immediately to offer God his son? He was able because he trusted. His subjective trust was real enough to find objective expression in his choice to obey. In this union of the subjective and objective dimensions of life we are given a clear illustration of what the Bible means when we are invited to "believe on the Lord Jesus Christ."

Like Abraham, we are to trust God so completely that our whole way of living gives evidence of inner change. The Bible tells us that when Abraham did believe the promise, "It was credited to him as righteousness." God looked within Abraham and announced to all, "This man is now righteous through faith." But how can such a pronouncement be justified? How could Abraham's claim to be made righteous by God's action be proven? The proof came when God spoke and Abraham obeyed. The proof came when Abraham's behavior testified to that inner transformation which God had preannounced.

So we need to examine our own claim to have faith today. Do we believe that Jesus lived and died for us? Well and good. But have we trusted ourselves to Him? If we have, we hear God's pronouncement that our trust has been credited to us for righteousness. If we have, we will increasingly discover that our claim to trust is being demonstrated objectively by obedience to God's Word. Trust in God will increasingly find expression in unhesitating response to God.

And so the story of Abraham moves beyond history and slips into today. The Genesis report challenges us today: What is my relationship with God? Is it like Abraham's, based on trust in God's promises and on confidence that He is trustworthy? Is my faith a living one, expressed in increasing obedience to God?

Thus the story of Abraham presents us with a divine invitation. In this purposive universe of ours which is moving surely toward its appointed end, God is not so concerned with His cosmic purposes that He neglects individuals. No, you and I are objects of His deep concern. Because He cares for us as individuals, God has given us a special promise in His Son. Jesus, who is the long-awaited King, has stooped to wear a crown of thorns and to be nailed to a bloody cross before He takes the throne. God's Word comes in explanation: "God so loved the world, that he gave his only begotten Son, that whosoever believeth in him should not perish, but have everlasting life" (Jn. 3: 16, KJV).

That "whosoever" includes you.

And me.

In Jesus Christ each of us is invited to repose in Abraham-like trust. In Jesus Christ you and I are

153

promised full forgiveness and transformation.

Let's respond to His word of promise just as Abraham did so long ago. Let's trust God. Let's accept God's gift of righteousness.

GOING DEEPER

to personalize

1. Abraham's kind of faith works in others besides the patriarch. Study Genesis 24 to see how Abraham's servant demonstrates both subjective and objective faith.

From your study of this chapter, write a description of your own life, showing how it is characterized as one lived "by faith."

2. Develop two lists expressing your own experience. On the one list include: Ways I know my faith in God is Abraham's kind. On the other list include: Ways other people know my faith in God is Abraham's kind.

What does the making of these two lists tell you about yourself?

3. Read Romans 4 carefully again, and write down any questions you would like to raise or any insights you would like to share in class.

4. Finally, look at Hebrews 11: 1-3, 6. From these verses write your own definition of faith.

to probe

1. Study these New Testament passages which draw on Abraham's life and experience, and write

a summary of what each is saying, using your own words: Romans 4; Galatians 3: 15—4: 7; James 2: 14-26.

2. Do a paraphrase of James 2: 14-24 to clarify and remove the "contradiction" some feel they see in this passage with the rest of the Bible's teaching about justification by faith.

11

SELAH

WE MEET THAT WORD *selah* in the Psalms. There it has the impact of a "rest" in a musical score. Stop a moment. Pause.

"Selah" is an appropriate title for these chapters in Genesis. They tell the story of the son and grandson of Abraham, men to whom the Covenant was confirmed and through whom the Covenant line is traced. But their lives mark a pause in the development of the divine purpose. No great and single message shines through these chapters as it did through the earlier sections of Genesis. In Abraham God introduces the Covenant theme which dominates the Old Testament. And Abraham represents all who throughout the ages will find a relationship with God through faith.

But Isaac and Jacob are lesser men, and consequently play less significant roles. Yet, like all "less significant" people, they are easier for you and me to identify with. In God's dealings with them, we can find much to enrich our own lives.

STUDYING THE OLD TESTAMENT

There are many approaches to take in studying
Scripture. Each has its purpose and function. Each
is appropriate; each gives us insight into the meaning and message of the sacred text.

Among the ways we might study Genesis 25—36
are these: the archaeological, the theological, the
devotional and what we might call the comparative: looking at the rest of Scripture to see what
God selects to emphasize.

The archaeological. This approach involves examining the customs and folkways of Bible times to
help us understand actions reported in Scripture.

This method is helpful on two counts. First,
we're kept from reading motives and causes into
the actions of Bible characters which really are not
there. For instance, in Genesis 31 we read that
Rachel, Jacob's wife, stole her father's household
gods (idols). Perhaps an immediate reaction is,
"Ah ha! The family is involved in pagan worship,
and Rachel wants to hold onto her religion. The
family may be going back to Palestine, but Rachel
will continue to be a pagan." I'm sure that sermons
must have been preached on this text, on the
danger of bringing along our old "gods" when we
turn to Jesus and journey toward our own "promised land."

There's only one problem with such an application. The interpretation of Rachel's action is in er-
ror. In those days the household gods were a sym-
bol of family headship. The heir was the one to
possess the household gods. When Jacob fled with

his family, Rachel's theft was her way of laying claim for her husband to all that her father had. It's possible that this theft and the claim it implies were major factors in leading Laban and his sons to pursue Jacob so far.

Archaeology also gives us insight into Jacob's "gift" to Esau when he sent herds of animals on ahead to his brother (Gen. 32, 33). When the two brothers met, Esau at first politely protested that he had plenty and did not need the gifts. Jacob urged him to accept. This urging was not from mere politeness, nor even a salve to a guilty conscience. In Jacob's time, to refuse such a gift would have meant that Esau was declaring himself to still be an enemy. Acceptance of the gift bound Esau to friendship. It was a visible sign to all that the brothers were truly reconciled.

Without some knowledge of the customs of Bible times, it is dangerous to make hasty judgments about the meaning or application of such incidents. We're too inclined to read into them meanings that are not there.

The second value of the archaeological approach to the study of a passage is found in the way that the Biblical record is confirmed. The customs are those of Palestine or Egypt, or wherever the location is, at just the time when the events took place. We are compelled to believe that, whatever else the Bible may be, it is an accurate record. It is a historical document in which we can have full confidence.

The theological. When we look at a portion of

Scripture from a theological perspective, we're concerned about what it reveals of God and/or His ways.

If we look at Genesis 25—36 this way, our attention is drawn at once to the centrality of the Covenant. After Abraham dies, God speaks to Isaac. He tells him to stay in Palestine and promises, "I will fulfil the oath which I swore to Abraham your father" (Gen. 26: 3). The obedience of faith had kept Abraham in the place of blessing; now Isaac is exhorted to trust and obey, and assured that through his line the original promise will be kept.

An express personal promise is communicated as well. God promises to be with this man, Isaac, to bless him (26: 3). God is not making a new covenant. The Covenant has been established with Abraham. Abraham's descendants are simply invited to participate in it; there is no need to constantly remake a promise once given.

It's the same with Jacob. Isaac, Jacob's father, blesses him as inheritor of the Covenant. (Note: archaeological discoveries indicate that a father's deathbed blessing had the force of a will in patriarchal times.) Then God appears to Jacob, identifying Himself as "the God of Abraham your father and the God of Isaac" (28: 13). In this appearance God tells Jacob that the promises are now given to him; he is the heir and inheritor. Then, while returning to the Promised Land after being away 20 years, Jacob calls on God as the Covenant-keeping God (32: 9-13), and God appears to him, again reconfirming the Covenant promises (35: 9-15).

These repeated affirmations of the Covenant promise to Isaac and Jacob make it clear that the announced purposes of God will be fulfilled through the family line, a line that has its source in Abraham both as its physical progenitor and as an example of faith.

In these passages we see that God is working out His promises. The purpose is sure, restated to each generation of patriarchs. The land, the special relationship with God, the blessing and being a blessing are the very root of each generation's sense of identity. These are a people chosen "for my servant [your father] Abraham's sake" (26: 24).

The theological approach, then, allows us to keep the main emphasis of a section of Scripture in view. It lets us trace what God is doing and what He views as important by noting the repeated concepts and the personal interventions of God which give us our clues.

The comparative. In this approach to the study of a section of Scripture, we look at other parts of the Bible to find some divine commentary. What application has the Holy Spirit made of incidents recorded here?

Both direct and indirect applications are made in the Old and New Testaments of earlier incidents. The main theme of a passage may be directly commented on, as in Romans 4 where Paul examines the meaning of Abraham's experience with God which makes him the father of all who believe. At times, incidents may be pointed out as illustrations of principles which are not themselves the central message of the earlier passage. This is an indirect application.

For instance, in Romans 9 Paul looks back to the patriarchs to demonstrate a point he is arguing. It seems that some Jewish people in Paul's time have looked at Christianity as an implicit rejection of the Covenant and the Covenant people. They could not believe that God would abandon His promises, so they rejected this new faith in Jesus as the long-promised Messiah.

In answer, Paul points out that not every Hebrew is a spiritual descendant of Abraham, even though he may be able to trace his physical descent to him. Isaac and Ishmael were both Abraham's children, but God said the Covenant promise applied only to Isaac's seed. A reader may object to this point, since Ishmael was also the son of a slave. But Paul goes on to point out that Isaac fathered and Rebecca bore twins: Jacob and Esau. Yet God chose Jacob and rejected Esau, even before the boys were born!

The point is made. God has freedom to choose some as recipients of the Covenant blessings while rejecting others. And this choice does not in any way indicate a repudiation of the Covenant. Nor does God's decision to extend the benefits of the Covenant to Gentiles repudiate the promise to Abraham. The Gentiles who believe in God find a relationship with Him through faith just as Abraham did, thus fulfilling the intention of God that in Abraham all the nations of the earth should share in the blessings.

This then is an indirect use of the Old Testament. The main message of the Genesis record is not that God is free to choose those who benefit under the Covenant. But historical events demonstrate that God does make just this kind of choice, and that the Covenant itself is not violated by the selection of some but not all of Abraham's descendants as beneficiaries.

The Covenant was made with *Abraham.* Those who, like Abraham, have faith, are invited to share its blessings. Even an entire generation's unbelief could never invalidate the promise and the purpose of the Lord.

DEVOTIONAL STUDY

This is a very important and helpful approach to Bible study, one we all need to learn. In a way it builds on the comparative approach we've just seen.

In Romans 9 Paul goes back to Genesis and focuses on two incidents that illustrate how God deals with people. In devotional study we do something very similar. We fix on an incident and think about it. We ask, "What can I learn here about God's ways of working in my life?"

This is what sets the devotional approach apart from some of the others. Our primary concern is personal application. We want to enter into the experiences of men and women of the past, to see mirrored in their experiences with the Lord, God's ways with us. We find warnings in their faults, encouragement in their faith, hope in God's faithfulness to them. As all of these experiences are applied to our daily lives, our own lives are enriched and our confidence in God grows.

Let's look then at several incidents in these chapters to see how they might be approached devotionally.

Esau's hunger (Gen. 25: 29-34). Esau was the oldest son of Isaac and, according to law and custom, was in line to inherit all Isaac possessed, including the Covenant promise of God. This was his right by birth.

But one day after a hunting trip Esau came home hungry. Jacob was boiling a stew of lentils, and Esau asked for some. Seeing his chance and knowing his brother well, Jacob demanded Esau's birthright in return. The Bible tells us that Esau "despised" his birthright and swore it to Jacob as the price of the pottage.

What a picture! Esau weighed the promise of God's continual presence and blessing against a bowl of soup—and valued the soup more highly. What a revelation of Esau's character. He was a man who valued the present rather than the future, the material rather than the invisible. The momentary satisfaction of physical desires seemed more important to him than the approval of God. The body, not the spirit, dominated his scale of values.

I can look at Esau's act and be amazed at it. But

what I need to realize is that this act of selling the birthright was an action which was in character rather than out of character. It was the result of a long process of character formation, a long history of choice after choice which shaped Esau's personality.

Right now I may look at Esau with wonder and say, "I'd never do that." Instead I ought to look at the action as an expression of character and wonder: In what direction are my daily choices leading me? Do I so value my present experiences that I fail to discipline myself to wait when waiting is best? Do I have to have the pleasures of eating despite the fact I'm overweight? Do I choose for cash value now, though I'm giving up strict honesty? Is God high enough on my priority list to cause me to spend time with Him, or do other things push Him out of my thoughts?

I can shake my head in wonder at Esau, but I had better realize that unless I make a daily habit of rejecting Esau's values, I might someday be faced with a similar choice—and make the wrong one!

The stolen blessing (Gen. 27). Rachel and Jacob, her son, plotted to deceive Isaac and get the blessing for Jacob that Isaac wanted to go to his oldest son, Esau. Disguised to fool the now blind Isaac, Jacob stood before his father and lied, "I am Esau your first-born" (27: 19).

How completely unnecessary! At the brothers' birth God had told Rachel that the older would serve the younger (25: 23). Yet as the critical time drew closer and closer, mother and son felt called to "help out God."

What was the result? Jacob did receive the blessing which he would have received anyway. Bitterness was heightened between the brothers, and Esau's hatred was so intense that he planned to kill his brother after their father died. Their mother, who plotted to help her favorite son, was forced to send him away for 20 years and did not live to see him return.

True, it worked out in the end. But the anger, the fear, the separation—all these might have been avoided had Jacob and Rachel simply trusted God and rejected deceit.

There are two important lessons for me here. First, I need to realize with gratitude that God can overcome my past failings and even use my mistakes to fulfill His purposes.

Second, and more importantly, I don't have to take Jacob's route to blessing! Instead, I can trust God and commit myself to do the right thing at all times. Truth, not lies, will serve me far better. God's will still will be done, and I'll be able to live in harmony with those around me. How great it is to shrug off all sense of pressure and to commit my way to God, confident that as I daily do His will, His good purposes will be performed.

Jacob's prayer (Gen. 32: 9-12). After 20 years with his father-in-law, Laban, Jacob took his wives and children and flocks to return to the Promised Land. God told him to return, but he was frightened. The remembrance of the wrong he'd done

Esau 20 years ago as well as Esau's hatred combined to produce guilt and terror.

Now Jacob is about to meet his brother. Driven to the Lord, he prays the longest recorded prayer up to this time. It's fascinating to see what Jacob says. He reminds God of His Covenant promise (vs. 9). Then he denies any personal merit as a possible basis for God's favor and reminds God (and himself) of the blessings from God he has enjoyed (vs. 10). Then he honestly admits his fear of Esau and begs God's help (vs. 11). Finally he reminds God of His personal promise to him that his descendants would be the chosen people (vs. 12).

In many ways Jacob's prayer is a model for me. I have to give up all notion of personal merit as a basis for claiming God's favor. I can and must rely on the character of God as a Covenant-keeping God, One who keeps all His promises to His people. I need to be honest in expressing my fears and doubts and uncertainties to God, to face my own deep need of Him and Him alone for strength and provision. Also I need to remember God's personal promises to me as one of the "whosoever" for whom Christ died. Because in Jesus God has freely given me all things, I can know that He seeks only to do me good. Because of who God is, I can abandon everything to Him. And rest.

The wound of grace (Gen. 32: 24-32). On the night Jacob prayed, he went out to plan his own way to gain Esau's favor. He prepared a number of gifts for his brother and sent them on ahead. He trusted God—and then took out insurance.

167

That night a "man" whom Jacob assumed to be an angel or theophany (a preincarnate appearance of God in human form, vs. 30) wrestled with him. In the struggle, the man touched the back of Jacob's thigh. Some commentators feel the ball and socket there were thrown out of joint. Others say that a ligament (sinew or tendon) was torn. Jacob was left with a permanent limp.

Sometimes a wound is a very special act of God's grace. Jacob struggled to hold onto the man, for after suffering the wound he must have realized how much more powerful this visitor was than he himself, and he wanted his blessing.

How often I need to be wounded for the same reason! It's easy for me to trust my own skills and abilities. But sometimes a wound (physically, or in a broken relationship, or the failure of a much-loved plan) will remind me to cling to God again, totally dependent on Him for blessing. How good it is that God doesn't hold back from hurting me—for my own good.

In this experience Jacob received a new name: Israel, "he who strives with God." Jacob had struggled with God, refusing to give up until God blessed him. That name may well represent the transformation of character that had begun in Jacob's past. But now that the wound remained, a constant reminder would be crystallized and confirmed. A Jacob fully dependent on God can become an Israel. What can I become if I let each wound draw me closer to the Lord and make me more dependent on Him?

GOING DEEPER

to personalize

1. Read rapidly (as a novel) Genesis 25—36.
2. Review the passage again and pick several incidents you would like to explore devotionally. Then select three and write out your thoughts (as in pp. 163-168). Be sure to include what these mean to you.

to probe

1. Use a concordance to locate Old Testament comments on characters or incidents reported in Genesis 25—36. Record the applications made by the inspired writers.
2. Use a concordance to locate New Testament comments, and do the same as above.

JOSEPH

WITH THE STORY OF JOSEPH, the plot of the Old
Testament once again begins to unfold. God told
Abraham, "Know of a surety that your descendants will be sojourners in a land that is not theirs,
and will be slaves there, and they will be oppressed
for four hundred years; but I will bring judgment
on the nation which they serve, and afterward
they shall come out with great possessions" (Gen.
15: 13, 14). In Joseph we see God preparing the
way for His people to leave the Promised Land
and to grow far greater in Egypt than they could
have done had they remained in Palestine.

The story of Joseph has fascinated laymen and
scholars for centuries. As a man, Joseph is one of
the Bible's most commendable characters, and his
experiences remind us in many ways of Jesus. As a
historical record, the portrait given in Genesis of
life in Egypt has been demonstrated to be amaz-
ingly accurate—amazing at least to those who used

to argue that Joseph's story was written a millennium or so after the supposed events. Leon Wood summarizes some of the details which ring so true:

> Corroboration of details in this over-all story with contemporary Egyptian practices and customs illustrates the accuracy of the Biblical record. The titles, "chief of the butlers," and "chief of the bakers," occur both in Genesis (40: 2), and extant Egyptian texts. Famines were known in Egypt and the idea of persons being assigned to dispense food during these famines is borne out in tomb inscriptions. One inscription speaks even of a seven-year famine at the time of the Third Dynasty (2700 B.C.). Indication is made on the Rossetta Stone that the Pharaoh had a custom of releasing prisoners on his birthday, as he did the butler (Gen. 40: 20). Joseph shaved before seeing Pharaoh (Gen. 41: 14), and shaving was a distinctive practice of Egypt. Pharaoh gave Joseph a signet ring, linen clothing, and a gold chain (Gen. 41: 42), all three of which are mentioned in Egyptian texts for similar use. Some scholars have objected to the idea of Joseph, a Semite, being elevated to such a high position in Egypt; but a letter dating from the Amarna period has been found written to a person in similar position having the Semetic name Dudu (David). It fits, too, that the Twelfth Dynasty, ruling at this time, has now moved the capital back from Thebes to

the northern site of Memphis. Joseph was thus more accessible to his brothers coming down from Canaan, as the continuing story indicates, and also to them living later in Goshen after Jacob's arrival.[1]

THE MAN AND HIS MISSION

Joseph, the son of Rachel, his father Jacob's favorite wife, was younger than the sons of the other wives. The Bible says that Jacob loved Joseph more than his brothers, and showed open favoritism (37: 2-4). As a result the brothers hated Joseph and were constantly critical and cutting in speaking to him.

At seventeen Joseph had dreams which indicated he was to have authority over his brothers and his parents. He foolishly told the dreams, and while his father took them seriously, the brothers became more jealous. A short time later Joseph was sent to make sure that all was well with his brothers, who were herding the family flocks on a distant range. Seeing Joseph approaching, the brothers conspired to kill him but were restrained by Reuben. When a trade caravan of Midianites passed nearby, they decided to sell Joseph as a slave instead.

It's hard to imagine Joseph's feelings at this time. His own family had rejected him, plotted to kill him and, in fact, had sold him to be a slave in a foreign land. We could hardly blame this teenager

1. Wood, pp. 78, 79.

if he had simply given up and surrendered to despair.

But, in fact, when Joseph was sold in Egypt to Potiphar, a high Egyptian official, he actively applied himself to serving. He became so successful that he was advanced to oversee all of Potiphar's affairs. And "the Lord blessed the Egyptian's house for Joseph's sake" (39: 5).

But Joseph had attracted the attention and passion of Potiphar's wife, who tried many times to seduce him. Joseph resisted, unwilling to sin against his master and against God (39: 7-9). One day when Joseph entered the house alone, Potiphar's wife literally tore his cloak from him. Joseph fled. Convinced now that she would never have Joseph, the scorned wife lied to her husband. As a result Joseph was stripped of his position and thrown into political prison "where the king's prisoners were confined" (39: 20).

Again Joseph might have lost heart. But again he approached the situation with perseverance, and his capabilities won him quick advancement. In time Joseph became supervisor of the prison under the head jailor, and again the Lord prospered his activities.

In prison Joseph met two high court officials, the chief butler and the chief baker, and interpreted dreams for them. One was to be restored to Pharaoh's favor and the other to be executed. Joseph's God-given interpretations came true. Two years later when Pharaoh had puzzling dreams, his chief butler remembered Joseph, who was brought to the palace to interpret. Joseph explained that the dreams of Pharaoh were a warning from God of a great famine to follow a time of great plenty. Joseph proposed that a wise man be appointed to gather and store food during the time of plenty and then administer its distribution during the famine years. An impressed Pharaoh responded, "Since God has shown you all this, there is none so discreet and wise as you are; you shall be over my house, and all my people shall order themselves as you command" (41: 39, 40).

God had brought Joseph to Egypt as a teenage slave; now, at 30, he was exalted to the second place in the kingdom.

The rest of the Joseph story traces the trips of his brothers to Egypt during the famine years to buy grain. They confront Joseph but do not recognize him. After several visits Joseph reveals himself to his brothers, urging them not to be afraid. For Joseph realizes that "God sent me before you to preserve life . . . to preserve for you a remnant on earth, and to keep alive for you many survivors" (45: 5-7). Looking beyond the brothers' sinful motives, Joseph realizes that it was God, not they, who had ordained his sojourn in Egypt. This realization has removed all bitterness from Joseph's heart.

Joseph then has the entire family, more than 76 persons, come to live in Egypt, and he sets aside a fertile area for them. After the death of Jacob, whose body is returned to Palestine for burial, the brothers still fear Joseph and expect revenge.

They cannot understand this man whose willingness to do the will of God has given him joy even in suffering. Again Joseph reassures them: "You meant evil against me; but God meant it for good, to bring it about that many people should be kept alive, as they are today." And with this explanation Joseph promises to provide for them and their little ones (Gen. 50: 20, 21).

The last paragraph of Genesis reveals even more of Joseph's faith. He relies on the Covenant of God. Someday God will visit the family and take them again to the land sworn to Abraham and Isaac and Jacob. At that time, Joseph decrees that his people should carry his coffin with them on their return journey. Joseph's life had been lived in a land that, for all his power, was a land of exile. His body would lie, awaiting the final fulfillment of the Covenant, in the dust of the Promised Land.

There are many riches to explore in these chapters. It is particularly fascinating to study Joseph's character. No matter how discouraged he must have become at the many reversals he experienced, we never see Joseph doing less than his best. In crisis experiences we see him choosing to do what is right. Rather than being eaten up with bitterness against his brothers, or returning hatred for hatred, Joseph looks beyond them to see the hand of God. And he remains sure that God's hand is on him "for good."

How often we look at our tragedies as injustice, or as punishment for some unknown fault. We need more of this man's kind of trust in the loving goodness of God. God sometimes leads His children into suffering, but it is always done in order that He might bring good through suffering.

TYPOLOGY

In chapter 11 we looked at several ways to study the Old Testament. The story of Joseph leads us to consider another way: the typological.

A *type* is an event, character, or institution which has a place and purpose in Bible history but which also, by divine design, foreshadows the future.

For instance, Christ is sometimes called the "second Adam," and Adam himself is spoken of in Romans 5: 14 (NIV) as "a pattern of the one to come." There is no exact correspondence here. Yet Christ and Adam are alike in that each is the head of a race: Adam of sinful man; Christ of redeemed man. In regard to headship, Adam as the source of humankind foreshadows Jesus, the source of mankind's transformed brotherhood.

Another type is seen in the Passover lamb, the animal whose blood was sprinkled over the door of Jewish households at the time of the Exodus. When the angel of death saw the blood on the doorposts, he passed over the blood-protected home. So I Corinthians says, "Christ, our Passover lamb, has been sacrificed" (5: 7, NIV). The helpless lamb, whose blood bought safety for an Old Testament generation, speaks to us of Jesus' blood as well.

A type, then, bears some resemblance in function or meaning in the original historical setting to something or someone yet to come.

Some Bible teachers have gone overboard in seeking for types of Christ or Christian doctrines in the Old Testament. So we want to be careful in seeking typical significances. We never, for instance, build doctrine on types. What we do is study carefully a historical setting for a basis of typical meaning. At times we'll find areas of strong resemblance between Old Testament events or persons and features of the New Testament. And these correspondences will help us appreciate the meaning of truths which stand constant through the sweep of history as central elements in God's plan.

But why speak of types and typology here? Because most Bible students have seen in Joseph's life and mission many parallels to Christ. Rejected by his brothers, sold for silver, suffering in a foreign land for the good of those who betrayed him, Joseph does bear a striking resemblance to the Savior. And Joseph's forgiving spirit also foreshadows the attitude of Jesus, who one day would cry from a cross, "Father, forgive them; for they know not what they do" (Lk. 23: 34).

TO EGYPT?

The story of Joseph does more than give us a portrait of a man of great faith and admirable character. It also marks a major turning point in the history of God's chosen people. Israel moves from the Promised Land to Egypt, where, after a time, Joseph will be forgotten and the people enslaved.

Why was Egypt part of God's plan for His people? In the next book in the **Bible Alive Series,** *Freedom Road,* we'll look in depth at all God taught His people through their enslavement and through His great acts of redemption. But even now we can see several reasons why the Hebrews needed to leave Palestine and spend centuries in Egypt. Leon Wood summarizes:

> Egypt was a country in which Jacob's descendants would have to remain a separate people, for Jacob and his sons were shepherds, and shepherds were an abomination to the Egyptians (Gen. 43: 32; 46: 34). The fact would remain a natural barrier to intermarriage. In Canaan there had already been some intermarriage with the inhabitants and continued living there would have brought more. This could only have led to serious amalgamation with the Canaanites, rather than distinctiveness as a nation. Further, Egypt afforded excellent living conditions for necessary rapid growth in numbers. The land of Goshen was fertile and regularly watered by the flooding Nile for adequate food supply.[2]

We might also point out that Canaan, during

2. Ibid., pp. 80, 81.

179

the centuries that the Jews were in Egypt, was a highway for the armies of nations to the north and south. The Hebrews could hardly have grown in numbers as they did in the protected environment of Egypt. In a very real sense, Egypt was a womb in which the seed of Israel grew and multiplied, until in God's own time a nation was born.

A glimpse of God's purpose in bringing Israel into Egypt helps us focus on the primary message of these Genesis chapters. Joseph himself sums up the message as he reassures his brothers: "God sent me before you to preserve for you a remnant on earth, and to keep alive for you many survivors. So it was not you who sent me here, but God" (45: 7, 8). What is the message? God is a Person who is in control of circumstances, who works providentially to accomplish His good purposes.

It's important that we grasp this truth about God as firmly as Joseph did. In Genesis we've seen God act in direct interventions. He created Adam and Eve. He set aside the orderly processes of nature to bring on earth a cataclysmic Flood. He spoke to Abraham directly. He acted in a clearly supernatural way to overthrow Sodom and Gomorrah.

But there is no record that God spoke directly to Joseph. Joseph had heard stories of the Covenant from his father. Joseph had dreamed dreams. But God did not meet with Joseph or confront him.

There is no record of God acting to set aside natural processes on Joseph's account. God blessed Joseph's efforts in Potiphar's house, in prison and in his position as a ruler of Egypt. But it was through Joseph's own honesty and efforts that the Lord worked. In the unfolding of circumstances, Joseph sees the hand of God. But certainly others would have seen only luck—both good and bad.

But Joseph's view is the true one.

As we trace through the rest of the Old Testament, we'll see that God sometimes intervenes directly. But in most cases God works through the ordering of circumstances: through the natural progress of events whose sequence nonetheless is patterned to shape history according to God's plan and will.

It's important for us to see that this same will is active in our circumstances. Each child of God is as important to Him as Joseph. Not because we have a task as great as Joseph's, but because we're just as precious to the Lord. Thus we have that great New Testament affirmation of God's control of circumstances for our benefit: "We know that in all things God works for the good of those who love him, who have been called according to his purpose" (Rom. 8: 28, NIV). Even tragedies such as Joseph experienced are meant for good. True, they may not lead us to a place of blessing in some earthly Egypt. But one day we will find our place as kings and priests to reign with the triumphant Christ.

In that day the pattern of our individual lives will be seen, woven into the great tapestry of the overall plan of our God: A plan that has in sharp focus the preservation of men for a life that extends far beyond the short span allotted you and me on earth. A plan that involves with eternity the fullest restoration in our personalities of the sharpened image of our God.

GOING DEEPER

to personalize

1. Write a biographical sketch of Joseph. Include experiences which shaped his character. Also explore Joseph's view of God as revealed in his statements about Him. What can you and I learn from Joseph's approach to life?

2. The interplay between Joseph and his brothers in Egypt (Gen. 42—45) is fascinating. Why do you think Joseph did and said what he did?

3. Genesis 44: 18-34 shows an apparent change in the brothers from their earlier readiness to get rid of Joseph to a present hesitancy to do anything to harm their father, Jacob. Yet, how much can we read into their actions here? Do a character sketch of the brothers, examining all that this extended passage reveals about them.

4. You'll find it fascinating also to do a typological study of Joseph, comparing him to Jesus. Use the following chart to record similarities between the two. Note that several similarities have already been suggested. Begin your record with these, and then add others as you discover them on the pages of Scripture.

JOSEPH	CHRIST

to probe

1. Genesis 49 contains Jacob's blessing of his 12 sons. This deathbed pronouncement is thought by most commentators to give a prophetic picture of each tribe's future history as well as a commentary on the character of each of the sons. Check several commentaries on Genesis to see the writers' explanations and comments on two of these prophetic blessings: verses 8-12 and 16-18.

2. After studying the life of Joseph, how would you say that the experiences of individuals today relate to the overall plan of God? Would you say that Joseph's experiences are typical of believers or atypical? Can we expect our lives to be so interwoven with God's purposes or not? Why?

"LET THERE BE LIGHT"

THESE EARLY WORDS of Genesis, "Let there be light," are appropriate. In a special way this first book of the Bible marks the dawn of understanding for mankind. The most basic questions that anyone can ask are answered for us here. With this book understanding begins to dawn because its words bring into perspective the shadowy outline of a redemption that men could only dimly perceive before God the Spirit spoke.

This doesn't mean that before Moses set down these words men were completely ignorant of God. The Book of Job shows that individuals and cultures did have a certain knowledge of God before. Job and his friends had information about God that came from their observation of the world, from oral tradition handed down across generations and from dreams and visions in the night. Job and his friends were convinced that God was just, that He expected men to live morally and that He rewarded the righteous and punished the evil. Job and his friends also recognized the frailty of man and that somehow sacrifice made expiation for human sin. So they offered blood sacrifices to God and prayed for forgiveness. Yes, we can certainly say that men of the ancient world retained much truth about God, passed on from generation to generation.

Yet Romans still affirms, "What may be known about God is plain to them, because God has made it plain to them. For since the creation of the world God's invisible qualities—his eternal power and divine nature—have been clearly seen, being understood from what has been made" (Rom. 1: 19, 20, NIV). All men have some knowledge of God.

The universal experience of mankind gives corroborating witness to the truth of these words. But the fact is that in every culture basic truths are dimly reflected. These truths may be distorted, but they are there!

The supernatural. For instance, all men seem to have an awareness that there are powers beyond themselves. It may be that they worship idols. It may be demons that they placate with sacrifices. It may be the strange powers residing in stones or trees that they fear. Or it may be some great abstraction, like that of Buddhism, that they revere. But in every society and culture there does reside a sense of something beyond.

Morality. All men also seem to have a sense of right and wrong. Oh, an individual may be amoral. But no society has been discovered in which moral codes are absent; in all, some actions are deemed morally correct and others morally wrong. Specific sexual taboos may differ from culture to culture, but in every society there is some code of sexual morality.

The gap. All cultures also show awareness that a gap exists between that which is felt to be right and people's actual behavior. In Western culture a sense of *guilt* most often marks failure to do what is believed to be right. In Eastern cultures it is more often a sense of *shame.* Yet all cultures show awareness of the inadequacies of individuals and their failure to live up to the moral ideals they espouse. Men and women fall short of being what they feel they ought to be.

However dim, the vestige of divine truth is there.

One night I went fishing on a familiar lake. I drove my 12-foot fishing boat along a cliffside shore, ready to turn into a bay where I often had fished during the daytime. Suddenly I seemed to have lost my bearings completely! There on the left loomed an island that I knew couldn't be there! At that moment, looking around, I felt I was on an absolutely strange sea! The dark shapes around me lost their friendliness, and the warm night took on a peculiar chill. The darkness had confused me; I felt lost and strange.

It must have been like this for mankind before revelation. The shadowy shapes of reality were there all along. They were even dimly perceived.

187

But because of the darkness that had fallen, the shapes could not be clearly seen. For such shapes to be understood, to be stripped of their aura of fear, men must await the dawn.

As the day began to dawn there on Saguaro Lake, I felt a flooding relief. In the delicate early light the black and formless shapes took on their familiar character. I realized that I had drifted from my course. Unknowingly I'd driven in a half circle, and the strange shape I'd taken for an island was a well-known peninsula jutting out across the shallow flats I'd planned to fish. When day began, the details of the shapes I'd feared became known. And, knowing where I was, I found peace.

It's just like this with Genesis. Mankind had retained a shadowy knowledge of God apart from revelation. But in the darkness the shapes took on a terrifying and awesome character. The meaning of what was seen could not be clearly known, and men who since Adam's first denial of God had never been able to fully trust Him, shrank back in fear. Man was adrift now on planet earth, and all the blazing daytime light of Sol could never burn away the doubts and awful uncertainties that welled up in the night.

And so it has been for all of us—of every generation. Until we've opened God's Word.

Until day dawns.

DAWN

For anyone who chooses to explore these first

books of the Bible, Genesis marks the coming of a personal dawn. The shadowy·ideas we have about God are dispelled, and we discover truths about ourselves and God's universe which have the potential to bring peace.

Let's trace the development of Genesis and see again the basic questions answered here.

A personal universe. In the very first words of Genesis we discover that our universe is a personal one. Some take the position that the universe is impersonal, that life itself is an accident, the result of random couplings of mindless elements in incredibly ancient shallow seas. They have tried to find meaning in this explanation of the universe—and have failed. What can a momentary spark of life in a vast and mindless heap of inert matter ever mean?

But Genesis 1 affirms God: God, a Person who existed before the physical universe, and who created it! The living, not the inert and mindless, is the ultimate reality.

Moving beyond this affirmation, Genesis 2 introduces mankind. Again the soft light of dawn strips away the shadows and reveals you and me in a new light. We've been so aware of our weaknesses and sins, so aware that men who cannot believe in God have looked back to the beasts to explain themselves in some brutal origin. But Genesis points us to a different origin, an origin that affirms man's dignity and worth and asks us to begin our search for identity by seeking an explanation not for the evil in us but for the good. And

Genesis shows us clearly the source of that good: man was originally created in the image of God.

And man, in God's image, is special.

This revelation is a particularly important one. You and I can find no justification in ourselves for the belief that we are valuable and important. But in the story of Creation we make a startling discovery. Our worth is not related to what we do. Our worth is rooted in who we are. As the special creation of God, as persons made in His image, we are intrinsically valuable. Each human being, each life, is precious to Him.

And so two of the basic questions are already answered! Who am I? How am I to understand the universe in which I live? The dawning light of Genesis has settled these troubling questions for all who believe.

Genesis then moves on in chapters 3 and 4 to explain another great problem: the problem of evil. The first pair chose to sin and in that choice brought death to the race. The evidences of death are still with us. The crime, the brutality, the thoughtlessness, the fears, the jealousy and the strife are all evidences of the fact that men are spiritually dead as well as doomed to experience a physical decay. Sin, as inadequacy and as willful choice, gives constant testimony to our need of God.

The fourth great message of early Genesis is found in chapters 6—9. The story of the Flood and God's judgment on sin tells us that we live in a moral universe. In this universe, righteousness is required and the Personality behind it all is just.

Thus the first chapters of Genesis speak to us clearly about the personal character of the universe in which we live, and they help us understand ourselves.

■ God, a Person, is the underlying reality.

■ Human beings, made in God's image, are of ultimate value. Not all the gold or jewels of this creation can be weighed against the worth of a single man or woman or child.

■ Human beings, warped by sin, stand in deep need of a restored relationship with God.

■ God's just character demands that the problem of sin be solved, or that man experience the judgment which justice and morality demand.

With Genesis, day has begun to dawn and its light has made clear the shape of the universe in which we live. And it has shown us our place.

But, as Genesis also makes clear, the created order has been upset. We are out of step with the Creator. The Book of Job shows us man's struggle to relate to the great Personality behind the universe. Here we have no small voice shouting futilely in the face of an impersonal, uncaring universe. Rather, we have one man finding peace in his relation to God in spite of mystery and suffering. Job points the way for us to enter into the depths of relationship with God through trust.

A purposive universe. In the second half of Genesis the focus shifts. We are no longer dealing with the entire race. Now we see God choose a man, and God announces that through this man and his de-

FIGURE V   CHART OF THE PRIMEVAL AND PATRIARCHAL PERIODS

Chapters	Key Word	Theme and Message
Gen. 1	Creation	The universe is *personal*
2	man	Men are made in God's image
3, 4	sin	Sin introduces death's reign
6—9	judgment	The universe has moral order
Job 1—31	suffering	God's ways are a mystery
Job 32—42	trust	God is to be trusted
Gen. 12, 15	Covenant	God's promise reveals purpose in the universe
12—21	sinful	Abraham and all men fall short
12—24	faith	Faith in God is "counted . . . for righteousness"
25—36	transmission	The Covenant promise was transmitted through Isaac and Jacob
37—50	Egypt	God providentially orders events to work out His purpose

scendants He will accomplish specific purposes.

The first thing we note in Genesis 12—24 is that God has announced His purpose in the form of a promise. And that promise is confirmed as a Covenant oath (a contract). In the Covenant with Abraham, God explains that His plan will be worked out in specific ways. God will:

- make Abraham a great nation.
- bless Abraham and make his name great.
- make Abraham a blessing.
- curse those who curse him and bless those who bless him.
- through Abraham bring blessing to all mankind.
- give Palestine to Abraham's descendants.

Looking ahead, we've seen that this first expression of God's Covenant promise is developed in later Scriptures. In Jeremiah we saw that the blessing to mankind is related to redemption, to giving men a new heart which will be cleansed from sin. And we've seen that this is tied to a Descendant of David who will be both King and Savior.

Abraham's children grasped the importance of the Covenant. From that first promise has grown the identity of the Hebrews: They have believed:

- They are a chosen people.
- They are somehow the source of blessing for the world.
- They hold the title deed to Palestine and a special place in God's plan and purpose.

Unless we understand the root of all Hebrew thought in the Covenant, we can never understand the Old Testament. For the Old Testament is the story of the Covenant people and of history's sure march, fulfilling the promises of God.

But Abraham is significant in other ways as well. Abraham is more than a lens bringing God's cosmic purposes into initial perspective. He is also a lens through which we begin to see God's solution to our need for righteousness. You and I, like Abraham, have no righteousness of our own. We stand side by side with him in our need for forgiveness and redemption. What we can have is that one quality which God has chosen to accept in men and credit to us as righteousness: faith. When God spoke to Abraham, this man responded. He trusted God enough to act on His word. That kind of faith is accepted by God as righteousness.

The rest of Genesis traces the family of this man. The Covenant promise is confirmed to the chosen line: to Isaac—not Ishmael. To Jacob—not Esau. Then with the story of Joseph, the next step in God's Covenant plan is unveiled. The family of Jacob goes together into Egypt to wait there until from the more than seventy persons a nation of two million will be born.

In the story of Joseph we find the last great message of Genesis. God cares, and God is in control. God is in charge of every circumstance. And even where His hand is not directly seen, we can be sure of His presence, providentially ordering events for His own purposes and for our good.

With the close of Genesis we're deeply aware that the day has dawned.

The universe we live in is both personal and purposive. That purpose includes the sweep of history—and touches you and me. In God's concern for Abraham we find our heritage too. We see again that God cares about each human being. In His gift of righteousness we see God's personal invitation to each of us. Through faith in the One who created and planned it all and who sums up that plan in Jesus Christ, you and I can find our own personal dawn.

Our heritage. And our peace.

GOING DEEPER

to personalize

1. To fix the message of Genesis in your mind and to give you mastery of its contents, memorize the chart on page 192. You can do it easily; it will enable you to think through these early books.

2. Thinking back, which message of Genesis has the most personal meaning to you? Why?

3. Review the various methods of Bible study noted in chapters 11 and 12. Select a passage such as Genesis 22 and use as many of these methods as you can to probe for its message and meaning.

to probe

1. From memory, write a summary of the Book of Genesis, tracing the themes as they develop.

2. From memory, write a summary of the Book of Job, tracing its development.

I. PRIMEVAL PERIOD	CREATION Creation to Abraham	Genesis 1–11 Job
II. PATRIARCHAL PERIOD (2166-1446)*	COVENANT Abraham to Moses	Genesis 12–50
III. EXODUS PERIOD (1446-1406)	LAW Moses' Leadership	Exodus Numbers Leviticus Deuteronomy
IV. CONQUEST OF CANAAN (1406-1390)	CONQUEST Joshua's Leadership	Joshua
V. TIME OF JUDGES (1367-1050)	JUDGES No Leadership	Judges Ruth I Samuel 1–7
VI. UNITED KINGDOM (1050-931)	KINGDOM Monarchy Established Establishment (David) Decline (Solomon)	I Samuel 8–11 II Samuel 1–24 I Kings 1–11 I Chronicles II Chronicles Psalms Ecclesiastes Proverbs Song of Solomon

	PROPHETIC MOVEMENT	
VII. DIVIDED KINGDOM (931-722) Israel Elijah Elisha Judah	Two Kingdoms	*II Kings 1-17* *II Chronicles 10-29* *Jonah* *Obadiah* *Amos* *Hosea* *Micah* *Joel* *Isaiah*
VIII. SURVIVING KINGDOM (722-586)	Judah Remains	*II Kings 18-25* *II Chronicles 30-36* *Jeremiah* *Nahum* *Zephaniah* *Habakkuk*
IX. BABYLONIAN CAPTIVITY (586-538)	JUDGMENT Torn from Palestine	*Ezekiel* *Daniel* *Esther*
X. RESTORATION (538-400)	The Jews Return *400 Years Between the Testaments*	*Ezra* *Nehemiah* *Haggai* *Zechariah* *Malachi*

197